Basic Survival

A Beginner's Guide

David Nash
Foreword by James Wesley Rawles

Skyhorse Publishing

Skyhorse Publishing books may be purchased in bulk at special discounts for sales promotion, corporate gifts, fund-raising, or educational purposes. Special editions can also be created to specifications. For details, contact the Special Sales Department, Skyhorse Publishing, 307 West 36th Street, 11th Floor, New York, NY 10018 or info@skyhorsepublishing.com.

Skyhorse® and Skyhorse Publishing® is a registered trademark of Skyhorse Publishing, Inc.®, a Delaware corporation.

Visit our website at www. skyhorsepublishing.com

10 9 8 7 6 5 4 3 2

Library of Congress Cataloging-in-Publication Data is available on file.

Cover design by Tom Lau
Cover photographs: iStock.com

ISBN: 978-1-5107-2467-9
Ebook ISBN: 978-1-5107-2469-3

Printed in China

Contents

This book is dedicated to those pioneers that have come before. Nothing in the realm of human endeavor is built on the work of a single human.
I learn from others, and seek to add to that body of knowledge.
Hopefully, you, the reader, will learn from my efforts, improve them, and pass them on in a never-ending stream of self-improvement.
In my preparedness journey, I have been lucky to have access to books, and the words of authors have molded and shaped me into who I am today.
A quote that sums up my preparedness strategy comes from my favorite author, Louis L'Amour.

Long ago I learned that nothing gets done by wishing it, you have to do it.

Foreword

What you are holding in your hands may be one of the most important books that you will ever read. This succinct book, written for the average person, encapsulates some very important points about family and community preparedness. This book could literally save your life.

Because we live in an increasingly complex and uncertain world, and because governments have repeatedly proven themselves incapable of adequately responding to disasters, the centerpiece and key element in disaster planning is *you*. It is *you* who must plan and prepare. And it is *you* who must mitigate and react to threats in a well-reasoned way, or your family may become just another statistic. (Death statistics look sad when reading them in a history book, but their full tragic weight is not felt unless they are seen by someone who has stood at the graveside services of some of the victims.)

David Nash has done a great job of putting together all of the salient points about modern disaster preparedness, not overlooking discussions of micro and macro level events, short-term and long-term scenarios, and the distinction between rapid onset versus "slow slide" disasters. And he includes vital information on surviving everything from a deep economic depression to asteroid impacts and nuclear war. The information you need is all here in one package, thanks to David Nash's meticulous research.

Don't dismiss preparedness as "someone else's problem," and don't look at disasters as just "some bad things we see on television." Someday—most likely in the span of your lifetime—disaster will come visiting you, right in your town. Even if you live a fully righteous life, respect others, live within your budget, and live in a "safe" neighborhood, things could go sideways in the blink of an eye. When they do, the difference between life and death will come down to your preparedness—physically, intellectually, and emotionally. But if you've prepared properly then your chances of survival will be dramatically higher. Reading this book and then putting a preparedness plan into action will be crucial in changing those odds of survival.

Please take this book seriously, and develop your own disaster plans. Once you've read this book, you've been warned. There is no excuse but to then methodically prepare yourself, your family, and your neighborhood for whatever may come. Once again, it all comes down to *you*.

JAMES WESLEY RAWLES
Founder and Senior Editor of www.SurvivalBlog.com

Introduction

Many of us are worried about the future. Wars, disasters, emergencies, social unrest, economic impacts, food insecurity, and rumors about all of the above can cause a person a lot of worry. Worry can lead to fear. Fear can cause people to seek solutions.

The majority of people in the preparedness community are honest and caring individuals that genuinely want to help. I have found a few unscrupulous individuals that cash in on fear to sell bad information or cheap gear. Luckily those individuals are pretty rare, what you are more likely to find are honest folks that are trying to help but are naively passing on incorrect information.

I cannot count the times I have heard well-meaning people talk about "radiation pills," Mountain Dew glow sticks, and heating a home using clay pots and a tea light candle. The explosion of preparedness communities on social media has caused bad information to be spread much faster than good information.

Preparedness involves effort. It takes work. Understanding that potassium iodide protects the thyroid from exposure to radioactive iodine released in nuclear power plants takes more work than just buying a bottle and thinking it is a cure-all radiation pill. It's easy to watch a YouTube video and see someone pour household chemicals into a bottle of Mountain Dew and use a black light to make it shine. Actually conducting the experiment yourself to see if it will glow or prove it's a trick is harder. Doing the math to see exactly how much thermal energy is in a teal light compared to the energy needed to heat a room is too concrete. It is not fun to find out something can't work in real life. It is much easier to believe it does.

I grew up on a park; when I read a book on Indian lore or wilderness survival I had the freedom to experiment and learn by doing. When I joined the Marines, I found that my sergeant frowned upon wilderness survival experiments in the barracks. I got in the habit of feeding my experimental nature by reading instead of doing. After some years I started thinking because I read something I *knew* it.

Fast-forward a decade and I thought I was a survival expert. That is, until I needed to actually perform one of the skills I had read about time and again. Needless to say, I flubbed it up. I made up my mind after that I would start learning by doing. I created a list and started experimenting. To keep myself honest, as well as to share my journey with others, I began videotaping my actions. I soon realized that skills were transferrable, preparedness was useful, and that I was having a lot of fun.

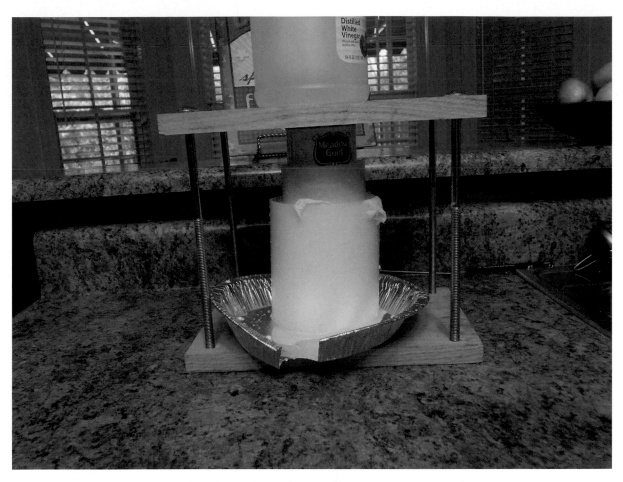

Making cheese was one project I thought was beyond me until I got practice, now it's fun.
Photo by the author.

As my skills improved, my confidence grew. I was able to take on more and more complex skills. After 10 years of experimenting I have a bunch of skills that I can rely on because I know they work. I have taken the time to learn the science behind why things are the way they are. Things that at one time seemed impossible are now easy.

This book is based upon decades of research, education, and practical experience. It is not the only way to prepare, and in the last section of the book I introduce authors, bloggers, and YouTube users that have their own ways of preparing for disasters.

I have learned from all of them. I don't discount their methods, but I find that the system I present in this book will work for almost any situation and almost every person. Because it is based on emergency management principles, it is easier to explain to those who don't yet feel the need to prepare because it is hard to dismiss someone as imbalanced for preparing for disasters if they are using terms and technology that originated with federal agencies created to deal with disasters.

Learn to Be Prepared—
Guaranteed

Being prepared is not impossible. It is not always easy, but anyone can cultivate a prepared mindset. Preparedness is about choices. A prepper chooses to spend time and resources to gain piece of mind. The motto of my training school is, "Don't be scared, be prepared."

An example of this would be earthquakes. Earthquakes pose a threat in my area. Rather than worry about them I took some time to prepare my home for earthquakes. A little education and some energy exerted gave me piece of mind. Before I took precautions I spent more time than I am willing to admit stressing over the potential destruction of a 7.2 or greater New Madrid Earthquake.

While I can guarantee that anyone can become more prepared for disasters, I cannot guarantee that the things you prepare for are the disasters that will occur.

In my work as an emergency manager, I have seen firsthand the devastation that a disaster can bring. Mother Nature can wreak havoc on a town. You have no choice in a tornado strike, the magnitude of an earthquake, or the suddenness of a flood. You do have a choice in how well you prepare for such events. You also have a choice in how you deal with those events.

I find that preparedness gives me confidence, it gives me choices, and it allows me to deal with a situation based upon the facts and not my fears.

I currently work full-time as an instructor. I love sharing knowledge, and helping other people grow and develop themselves and their personal skills.

Because I have seen the benefit of proper preparation on a personal basis I take great care in passing this knowledge on. This book takes the professional discipline of emergency management and incorporates the knowledge and skills from preppers to make a plan that is functional, practical, and realistic.

I find that many prefer to prioritize stuff over skills, but in reality, it should be the opposite. Having the mindset to survive is the base, with skills and responding appropriately to the situation based on that. Having the right materials is helpful, but they are the least important thing.

Basic Survival will help you prepare. It is a blueprint toward basic preparedness. When I started on the path toward self-reliance I did not have the benefit of a no-nonsense guide like this. I had to weed out the good knowledge from regurgitated information that the authors did not understand.

As an author I cannot make you use this book, but I can guarantee that I use the information within to keep my own family safe and that I have used each item contained here which was selected specifically to protect my own child. Because of that I am confident it will help you become better prepared.

In *Basic Survival* I will begin with the basics of academic emergency management as taught by the Federal Emergency Management Agency, United States Department of Homeland Security, and various universities throughout the United States. We will present some basic information on types of disasters, and some practical types of food, water storage, and basic first aid.

You will get a 19-step blueprint you can complete in less than three weeks that incorporates the information found in this book, and lastly you will find a resource section of books, websites, and YouTube channels that will give you some well-rounded additional study.

Four Phases of Emergency Management

If you want to truly prepare for disaster you need to take a systematic approach, otherwise you will risk preparing for the wrong things, preparing ineffectively, burning out, or just failing.

Academically, disaster response has been broken into four phases. Some of these phases blend into each other and don't always have a well-defined beginning and ending. By looking at preparedness through the lens of the four phases you can better understand what is going on and how best to deal with the situation at hand.

Those phases are:

- Mitigation
- Preparedness

- Response
- Recovery

Mitigation

Mitigation is the process of eliminating a threat, and if that is not possible taking action to limit the impact of that threat. It is generally the first aspect of emergency management because the best way to deal with a threat is to prevent it from ever happening.

Government mitigates threats by doing large-scale projects, like buying homes in areas prone to flooding and building parks.

For preppers, mitigation may be moving to an area not prone to disasters, buying insurance, storing fuel safely, and ensuring that bookshelves don't fall in an earthquake.

Mitigation activities tend to run hand in hand with preparedness activities, because things you can't prevent need to be prepared for.

In cyclical emergency management, mitigation also occurs toward the end of the recovery phase when rebuilding after a disaster allows for new designs and technology to be used to prevent the disaster from occurring again.

Going around the problem is much easier than fixing the problem.
Photo courtesy of iStock.com/sssstep.

Preparedness

Preppers tend to focus on the preparedness phase, and do not break up their actions into the four phases; however, preparedness is only one piece of the solution to becoming disaster-resilient.

In the preparedness phase, plans are made to response to an emergency. Those plans are tested, and the lessons learned from them go back into making better plans.

Additionally, once plans are made, resources are gathered to make the plans viable.

Gear is not bought simply because it is labeled tactical or has the term *survival* in its name. Each piece of gear has a part in the preparedness plan, is inventoried, tested, and trained on.

Training is accomplished in the preparedness phase. Having great plans is useless if nobody knows what they are or can't accomplish the tasks laid out in the plan.

When making plans, stay realistic and try not to make specific plans when a more general plan will suffice.

Keep in mind President Eisenhower's thoughts on planning: "In preparing for battle I have always found that plans are useless, but planning is indispensable."

Once you know what you have and what you need you should create plans to deal with threats with what you have. As you make these plans it is best to keep your plans generic as possible. In the emergency management world we call this "all hazards" planning. You do not need a specific food storage locker for a drought and a second for an earthquake. Canned tuna does not care what prompted you to open it. A plan for getting to your out of state sibling's house can work for a variety of events.

Some things need specific plans, and if this is the case feel free to create such plans, but the more generic and flexible your main plan is, the better you will deal with an emergency.

All Hazards Approach vs. Specific Threat Planning

A tendency many preppers have is to get really deep into prepping. It is a good feeling to take charge and to make changes that make you feel more safe and secure. This is evident in the planning for disaster response and reaction.

As a former emergency management planner charged with writing plans to deal with large scale emergencies, I understand the pull to make specific plans.

However, during his time as a General, President Eisenhower made his famous observation that plans were useless, it is the planning process that is essential.

What he meant was that during emergencies things go wrong. Items you planned for may not be available, the tornado may not follow the path you planned for, and the bad guy may not react like you rehearsed.

Rather than making specific plans for specific threats, it is better to take an all hazards approach whenever possible. I don't have a pantry of food for losing my job, another for earthquakes, and another

A well-stocked pantry works for a variety of disasters.
Photo courtesy of Salvation Army USA West.

just in case the other guy's candidate got elected. I have stored food. If I can't get to the grocery it is there when I need it. Why I need it is secondary.

Build a plan that is flexible and works for a variety of situations and you will be much better prepared than if you have a thousand complicated plans no one can remember.

However, that being said, there are specific threats that need some specialized planning. Some examples are:

- Hazardous Material/CBRNE (Chemical, Biological, Radiological, Nuclear, and Explosive) Threats
- Earthquakes
- Floods

These specific threats will receive special attention in the basic threats section.

Response

As with Mitigation and Preparedness, which are very similar with one phase beginning while the other is still occurring, Response and Recovery operate in much the same way.

In the response phase, the disaster has occurred and people have to deal with events that are out of their control. By definition, a disaster exceeds the ability to deal with it using the community's resources. That is a useful definition and allows for something to be considered a disaster in one place but not in another.

Disasters take many shapes and types, and it doesn't have to impact a large amount of people to be a disaster to you.
Photo courtesy of iStock.com/inhauscreative.

With that definition comes the chasing of resources. When the disaster occurs more things are needed than are available, but as responders begin to regain control and resources from other areas arrive, the disaster stabilizes and if more resources arrive, then eventually there are more materials in an area than are needed and at that point recovery officially begins.

Functionally, recovery can start much earlier, and in many cases, decision-makers keep recovery needs in mind as they begin response.

During the response phase, information is a key resource. Initial information is often wrong, confused, and fragmented. This makes decisions harder to make.

In order to keep track of actions and decision-making priorities, emergency managers use a system called LIPP Priorities.

LIPP Priorities

LIPP is an acronym that stands for:

- Life Safety
- Incident Stabilization
- Protection of Property
- Protection of the Environment

In a perfect world, decisions that are made would serve all of the above. Unfortunately, that is not how disasters work. If you have to make a decision, ensure that the decision will be in the best interest of saving lives. If possible get as many other priorities served by the decisions as you can. But don't let a lower level priority override the higher ones.

Stabilizing the incident is greater than protection of either property or the environment as long as the disaster is out of control and lives, property, and the environment are at stake.

Lives come first. Next we choose to protect property, and the environment is last.

Incident Command

One thing that FEMA (the Federal Emergency Management Agency) gets right is incident command. This is a system that allows for the smooth control of the multiple parts involved in disaster response. A Homeland Security Presidential Declaration mandated it after the 9/11 attacks.

The incident command system is based upon wildfire management systems that came from Marine Pacific war-fighting in World War II.

I find that the incident command principles readily adapt to being used in business, in event planning, and in personal disaster response with a team or a family.

Incident Command Principles

- Unity of command
- Span of Control
- Common terminology

Incident command can take many shapes, but it all involves managing resources and people to fix a problem. By Bob McMillan from the FEMA Photo Library via Wikimedia Commons.

- Management by objective
- Flexible and modular organization
- Incident Action Planning

Unity of Command

Everyone reports to only one supervisor; each person reporting to a single person eliminates getting conflicting orders from other supervisors. This increases accountability and improves coordination efforts.

The lead supervisor responsible for the disaster is called the incident commander.

Span of Control

With unity of command, span of control ensures that each supervisor is not overburdened with more staff than they can effectively manage. Each leader only has between three and seven direct reports, with five subordinates considered ideal. Each person only reports to one supervisor.

Common Terminology

Since the Incident Command System (ICS) is mandated for every responding organization that received federal funding of any sort, police, fire, EMS, public works, Hazmat response, animal control, and all other types of organizations use it.

Each organization brings its own terms, command structures, and methods of operations. ICS uses a single set of defined terms so that all responders are on the same page.

Management by Objective

Incidents are managed by working towards specific objectives. Objectives are ranked by the LIPP priorities and should be written as specifically as possible. The priorities must also be realistic, attainable, and time-sensitive.

These objectives are accomplished creating an incident action plan that outlines the basic framework of action and then building individual tactics to best meet the objectives.

Large scale disasters can take decades to recover from.
Photo By Greg Henshall, FEMA Photo Library.

Flexible and Modular Organization

The Incident Command structure can expand and contract as needed by the incident scope, resources, and hazards. The command structure is built from the incident commander down with positions only being activated as needed.

Incident Action Planning

Incident Action Plans (IAPs) ensure that everyone is working toward the same goals. At the end of each operational period (typically a 12-hour shift) the progress toward those goals are evaluated and a new plan is created to ensure the LIPP goals are being met.

I have taught Incident Command training for several years, and have seen how it makes an organized effort out of the chaos of a disaster scene. While I haven't taken it to the extreme, I have a coworker that used the incident command system to plan and manage a family trip to Disneyland.

There are free online courses in incident command, and I recommend taking the basic 100 level courses to everyone.

Recovery

Recovery is the phase where we try to get back to normal pre-disaster life. In this phase, the federal government may give grant funds or low cost loans to individuals and communities to rebuild.

For preppers, we restock, rebuild, mourn, and get on with life.

Recovery can take years; there are places that even now have not recovered from Hurricane Katrina.

In order to make plans, you need to have a grasp of basic threats your plan may need to address. The next section will introduce some basic threats found in North America.

Basic Threats In North America

I have twelve years of experience in state emergency management, and for several of those years I worked as an emergency management planner. I was "lucky" to work for Tennessee at that time because the state is situated in a way that causes it to have a multitude of natural disasters. It is common knowledge that some years Tennessee has more presidential disaster declarations than some other states have in a decade. I have worked floods, tornadoes, ice storms, hurricane relief, as well as hazardous material spills, factory fires, bomb threats, active shooter events, and nuclear power plant emergencies.

In the next section you will learn how to make plans for yourself, based on the same training I used to build governmental plans, but first you need to know the basic kinds of disasters.

Emergency Management doctrine involves grouping threats into two classes, natural and technological (man-caused) disasters. We will do the same.

Common Natural Disasters in America

Natural disasters are not controlled or caused by man. In insurance-speak they are sometimes called "acts of God." They are often unpredictable, brutal, and very damaging. They are mostly based on your geography and what one town may experience, another location may seldom or never face.

Drought

Droughts are common in the West, Midwest, and Southern US. Severe droughts impact our farming industry and are a common problem. In some places, droughts are so severe that the government has passed laws owning water and do not allow for rain catchment systems or changing creeks and streams on private land. In 2006, a National Integrated Drought Information System (NIDIS) was created to forecast and warn states of droughts.

In some places droughts are so severe that the government has passed laws forbidding rainwater collection. Photo by the author.

Earthquakes

Earthquakes are a common threat to citizens in the United States. Unfortunately, when people talk about earthquakes they immediately think of California. The New Madrid Fault is not as well known.

It can be argued that the well-known San Andreas fault in California is not nearly as dangerous as the New Madrid Earthquake that threatens the eight states of Arkansas, Illinois, Indiana, Kentucky, Mississippi, Missouri, Oklahoma, and Tennessee. This is due to the fact that the geology of the area around the New Madrid is prone to liquefaction. Liquefaction means the soil behaves like a liquid under earthquake conditions. This causes more destruction than mere shaking.

There is also a fault line that runs up the Appalachian Mountains that is highly active—so much so that nuclear power plants in the East are built with the fault line in mind. I used to work at an emergency operations center that had a computer linked to a worldwide seismic monitoring system. I watched this system detect earthquakes daily, however, we only average about four earthquakes a year that are strong enough to be felt.

Earthquake Response

During an earthquake, the procedure is to drop, cover, and hold on.

- Drop to the ground so that you will not be thrown off balance.
- Take cover under a heavy piece of furniture. If the building collapses, the furniture can create a small livable area that can protect you until help arrives.
- Hold on until the shaking stops. Once the quake is over, get outside to an open area and be aware of aftershocks.

Earthquake Preparedness

Many of the basic preparedness steps will help with earthquake preparedness. Having a 72-hour kit, being able to turn off your gas and electric lines to prevent fires, and having a communication plan are all important things to have in place before an earthquake.

Additionally you can:

- Secure heavy furniture such as bookshelves and dressers to the walls by strapping the rear of the furniture to a stud using heavy screws and webbing
- Use museum wax to secure decorative items such as vases and collectables to the shelves so that they do not fall off during violent shaking. Placing bungee cords around shelves holding canned food storage helps prevent breakage during a quake.
- Strap water heaters to the wall of the home; take care with gas lines to ensure the connections are flexible so that they do not break in an earthquake.

Drop, cover, and hold on.
Photo courtesy of Department of Foreign Affairs and Trade.

Floods

Floods are one of the most common natural disasters. They are also very destructive, not just in initial damage, but in mold and property damage long-term. I worked the 2010 Nashville floods, and remember the flash floods floating a mobile home down Interstate 24. As of early 2017, some people still have not been able to return to their homes due to damage from mold and the flood.

Like earthquakes, floods do not threaten everyone equally. The US federal government has flood plain maps that identify flood-prone areas and require insurance to live in those areas. In cases of extreme flooding, mitigation grant programs actually try to purchase flood-prone neighborhoods and turn them into green spaces to avoid a continual disaster cycle of flood, recover, flood, recover.

There isn't much you can do low-cost to prepare for floods other than buying sandbags. Unfortunately, after a flood, recovery is very expensive as mold very often destroys a home worse than the original floodwaters do.

During a flood response, be aware of floodwater threats. It is not just the high water that kills, but also any hazardous materials in tanks that have also become flooded. If you live in an area with septic tanks, the waste inside will contaminate the water.

Floods are highly dangerous threats.
By Stephen Yeargin via Wikimedia Commons.

Electrical lines may energize the water, and only a few inches of moving water can wash away a car. The best thing to do once you have notice of a flood is to get to higher ground.

Disinfect canned foods that were covered by floodwater with a 10 percent bleach solution before opening, and throw any other foods away. The risk of consuming contaminated items is just too great.

Heat Waves

Heat waves are a mix of extremely hot weather and high humidity. The eastern United States is commonly hit with this disaster. Many think that a heat wave is an inconvenience, but this is a life-threatening disaster that can take dozens of lives each year. It is particularly deadly to the very young and the elderly. Anyone that has ever suffered a heat injury can tell you how hard they are to recover from, and how rapidly they can develop.

Hurricanes

Hurricanes and cyclones form out over the ocean, and while these storms are very destructive, they fortunately do not always make landfall. The paths of hurricanes are closely watched along the Gulf of Mexico and the Atlantic coast each summer. Hurricane Katrina caused straight-line wind damage as far north as Memphis, Tennessee, and Hurricane Andrew significantly damaged a nuclear power plant in Florida.

Heat can be a killer.
By Peripitus via Wikimedia Commons.

Hurricanes don't always make land, but they are highly destructive.
By the National Oceanic and Atmospheric Administration via Wikimedia Commons.

Thunderstorms

Many people underestimate thunderstorms, but they are more dangerous than you'd think. Each year more than 10,000 severe thunderstorms hit the Midwest and Central United States. High winds can cause massive damage to homes and businesses. Lightning alone kills about eighty people each year. Often thunderstorms spawn tornadoes, a natural disaster in itself.

Tornadoes

Tornadoes strike the United States more than any other country. They most often hit an area encompassing Kansas, Nebraska, Iowa, Missouri, and South Dakota called Tornado Alley. But don't think that if you like outside of Tornado Alley you are safe. Many other states get tornadoes each year, and I have worked many deadly tornadoes in Tennessee. I had to take time off to go to bring supplies to my in-laws after the large tornado outbreak in Northern Alabama in April of 2011.

Wildfire

Wildfires are also known as brush fires and forest fires. Whatever the name, they are known for their size and speed. A wildfire can easily destroy several thousands of acres in just a few days. Large ones are common in the western United States. The disaster management system used to deal with disasters of all types was based upon wildfire response in California. If you have ever seen an out of control fire, you will respect the danger of wildfires. Fire protection is something every home should have a plan for.

Lightning kills approximately eighty people each year.
Photo courtesy of Flickr: Akulatraxas.

Tornadoes cause multiple disasters yearly.
By Greg Henshall, FEMA Photo Library via Wikimedia Commons.

Winter Weather

In Tennessee we often joke about bad drivers and grocery store runs. It seems like every time it snows, people want to make French toast because the grocery store sells out of eggs, milk, and bread. Winter weather is no joke, as it has stranded thousands of motorists that were unprepared. Many think winter

Wildfires are well known in California, but can occur in almost every state.
By John McColgan via Wikimedia Commons.

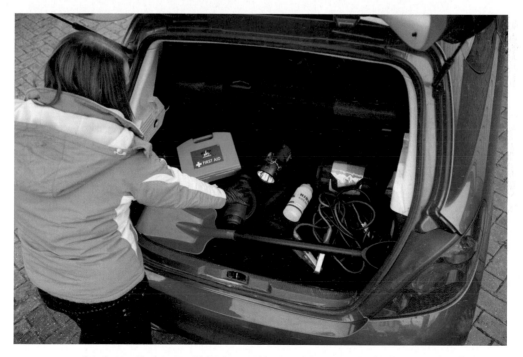

A winter car kit that includes wool blankets, sand or salt, and a shovel can be a lifesaver.
Photo courtesy of Highways England.

weather only impacts those in the Great Lakes states and the northeastern states but this is not true. The State Director of Georgia's Emergency Management Agency once resigned due to a poor winter storm response. A winter storm is a deadly combination of high wind speeds, blinding snow, and several days of snowfall. It doesn't take much ice to affect traffic, airports, and general life. Total damages from the three-day Groundhog Day Blizzard of 2011 were valued at $1 billion.

Volcanoes

Many Americans don't think about volcanic eruptions, but over the past one hundred years, the US has had almost three dozen eruptions. Volcanoes don't seem like a huge threat, considering most of them lie

When we think about volcanoes, we are conditioned to think about Hawaii, but they are are found in several US states.
Photo by Mike Doukas, USGS Cascades Volcano Observatory via Wikimedia Commons.

dormant, but they can quickly cause immense damage and destruction. The majority of these volcanoes lie along the West Coast, Alaska's coast, and Hawaii. People living on the East Coast may feel safe about Volcanoes, but an extinction level event could come from a super-volcano that lies under the Yellowstone National Forest.

Common Man-Caused Disasters in America

A technological hazard comes from technological or industrial conditions. This includes accidents, dangerous procedures, infrastructure failures, or specific human activities. Man-caused disasters may involve loss of life, injury, illness or other health impacts, property damage, loss of livelihoods and services, social and economic disruption, or environmental damage.

Dam Failures

In my state of Tennessee, every single lake except the one formed from the New Madrid earthquake comes from a dam. In recent years we had a huge issue because a dam near our capitol was in danger of collapsing. If you live near a dam you need to look at the flood inundation maps to see if a dam collapse will impact your house, and if so, how long will you have to evacuate. One of the first meetings I went to as an emergency planner was for a North Carolina dam. I learned that if the dam failed Tennessee would lose over a thousand people in less than fifteen minutes and there was not a good way to warn them as the majority of deaths would occur on our interstate as a wall of water collapsed the road in two places.

If you live downstream of a dam, you should have a comprehensive plan.
Photo courtesy of www.waterarchives.org.

Fire

Fire is interesting because it can be man-made or natural. It is a huge threat either way. When my son was an infant we had a kitchen fire. I remember the fear I had as I saw the flames and my child was in the house. A house fire is a devastating personal disaster; it can take lives and destroy a family's wealth in a matter of minutes. This disaster has no basis in geography so everyone should have a plan that involves prevention, detection, and escape.

Criminal Acts

Just because a criminal doesn't kill a mass of people does not mean it is not a disaster. I have had things stolen, and I have friends who have had family murdered. Having precautions in place to prevent and protect your family from crime is important in any comprehensive family plan.

Even a small kitchen fire can be a disaster.
Photo by the author.

Active Shooter

As a gun guy, I tend to focus on people-based threats; I gained certification as an Active Shooter Response Instructor because I feel I can do something about people a lot easier than I can nature. An active shooter event is when an individual is actively engaged in the murder or attempted murder of persons in a confined and populated area. An active shooter does not generally have a pattern or method to the selection of victim.

The Advanced Law Enforcement Rapid Response Training (ALERRT) Center teaches that In dealing with an active shooter you should:

- Avoid—In avoiding the active shooter you always have an exit plan, pay attention to your surroundings, quickly identify that the event is taking place, and get as much distance and as many barriers between you and the shooter as possible.

Avoid the shooter, deny him access, defend yourself.
By Petty Officer 3rd Class Lauren Laughlin via Wikimedia Commons.

- Deny—If you can't get away make it difficult to get to you. Barricade yourself away from doors and windows, turn off the lights, remain quiet and out of sight. Don't forget to silence your phone
- Defend—If you can't get away and you can't deny the attacker access, then be aggressive and fight to survive. Use whatever tactics and tools at your disposal. Nothing is off limits to defend yourself against an active shooter.

Terrorism

All terrorism is a criminal act, but not all criminal acts are terrorism. Fear drives much of the government response to terrorism, but fear is the goal of the act. Terrorists want to use fear to cause the government to change. In our modern world acts of terror will increase, as will the government's response. For the individual, education, vigilance, and the same protections against crime will be the citizen's best defense.

CBRNE (Hazardous Materials)

Depending on if it is intentional or accidental, as well as where and when a person trained, hazardous materials have several names: CBRNE, COBRA, Haz-Mat, or a WMD. Names don't matter to those in or near the oncoming green cloud of death. What matters are the concepts of how to protect yourself and your family from the toxic chemicals

Shelter in Place or Evacuate

In dealing with the release of a toxic chemical that can spread, no matter the type, there are two basic ways of protecting the public, Evacuation and Shelter in Place.

Evacuation is used when the public has the time and ability to flee ahead of the spread of the toxic plume. If you live near a transportation route like a interstate, railway, or waterway large enough for barge traffic, it makes good sense to keep a disaster kit packed, know the routes out of your neighborhood, and have a place to go. If an evacuation is ordered, time is precious. Get out as soon as possible. Additionally, having a communication plan for family not present to know how to find you is also useful in an evacuation. When an evacuation order is given, government officials typically set up shelters and will test the area before a return order is given.

Shelter in Place is when the public does not have time to flee, and must prepare to survive until the threat passes. If the order to shelter in place is given, close all the doors, windows, and ventilation openings to the outside of your house. Use plastic wrap and duct tape to seal them well. Additionally, turn off your air conditioner/heater so that contaminated outside air is not pulled into your home.

When the order to shelter in place is given, the response workers are on a clock. Air purity and heat/cold issues are on the decision-maker's minds. The thought is to clear the area and give the all clear as soon as possible so that the home can be aired out. Leaks in improvised seals can cause toxic agents to enter the home and concentrate over time, making the inside of the home potentially more dangerous than the outside under some circumstances. If a shelter in place order is given, be sure to rapidly and thoroughly seal your home, and to stay near a radio or TV to listen to updates.

Shelter in Place when you cannot evacuate.
Photo courtesy of iStock.com/BanksPhotos.

Chemical

There are millions of registered industrial chemicals with hazardous properties. These chemicals are shipped in bulk daily throughout our nation. During my time in a State Emergency Operations Center it was not uncommon to work 1,500 to 2,000 transportation accidents involving hazardous materials of some type annually.

Besides accidental release of toxic industrial chemicals, there is also the possibility of criminal release of toxic chemicals for terroristic purposes. Being able to recognize such an attack and rapidly leave the area can save your life. Sometimes a chemical release may not be immediately identifiable because the toxic agent may be colorless, odorless, or may not cause immediate effects.

Signs of a Toxic Chemical Attack/Release

- Droplets of oily film on surfaces
- Unusual dead or dying animals in the area
- Unusual liquid sprays or vapors
- Unexplained odors (smell of bitter almonds, peach kernels, newly mown hay, or green grass)
- Unusual or unauthorized spraying in the area

A plume is the cloud of toxic chemicals.
By Richard Chambers via Wikimedia Commons.

- Victims displaying symptoms of nausea, difficulty breathing, convulsions, disorientation, or patterns of illness inconsistent with natural disease
- Low-lying clouds or fog unrelated to weather; clouds of dust; or suspended, possibly colored, particles
- People dressed unusually (long-sleeved shirts or overcoats in the summertime) or wearing breathing protection particularly in areas where large numbers of people tend to congregate, such as subways or stadiums

If you see these or similar signs and you suspect an attack, get away—upwind and uphill are preferable. Many toxic chemicals are heavier than air, and if you can get to fresh air you can survive.

Biological

Biological attacks are similar in some ways to chemical attacks, but they generally take time for symptoms to become apparent. A person may be infected with a biological agent, but have no noticeable symptoms for several days or weeks until the organism replicates inside the victim's body and spreads enough to be symptomatic. However, there have been cases in which the initial exposure was so large that the patients were symptomatic within hours.

Biological agents are more sensitive to delivery methods; explosives generally kill the agents they are trying to spread. Many of the same signs of a chemical attack are the signs of a biological attack, but the animals and quick symptoms in a small area would point more to chemical, whereas an aerosol sprayer and the people in protective gear without immediate victims would tend to signal a biological agent.

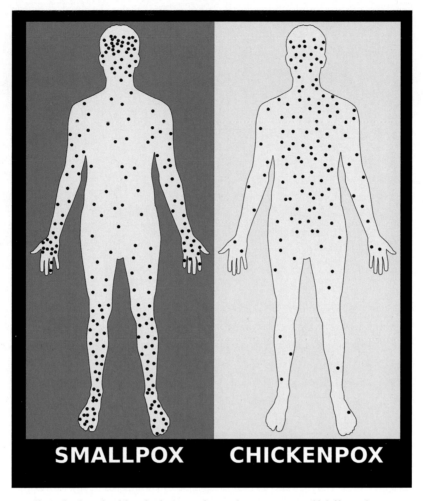

SMALLPOX **CHICKENPOX**

Smallpox looks a lot like chicken pox but it does present itself differently.
Author unknown via Wikimedia Commons.

Radiological

Radiation is a chemical property of a material, caused from an unstable material attempting to become more stable. There are a lot of misunderstandings and bad information in the preparedness world concerning radiological events. I spent three years as a full-time radiological response instructor and several more years as a hazardous material technician, and without any hesitation, I would state that I would rather work a radiological event than a chemical release.

Radiological events are more predictable than chemical releases. Safety precautions are more easily put into place.

Radiation is basically energy travelling through material. Light, heat, radio, and microwaves are all radiating out from their sources. Radiation is all around you, but that radiation is divided into two basic classes, ionizing and non-iodizing radiation.

Radiation that has enough energy to knock around atoms in a molecule and cause them to vibrate, but not enough to actually kick electrons out of the molecule, is referred to as "non-ionizing radiation." Examples of this kind of radiation include visible light and microwaves.

If the radiation is powerful enough to bounce electrons out from their atoms it is "ionizing" because it creates ions. When we think about "radiation" this is the type we normally think about.

Types of Radiation

There are several different types of radiation, but the three most related to our health and the most common are Alpha, Beta, and Gamma radiation.

Alpha radiation is a heavy, very short-range particle and is actually an ejected helium nucleus. Some characteristics of alpha radiation are:

- Alpha radiation is not able to penetrate human skin.
- Alpha-emitting materials can be harmful to humans if the materials are inhaled, swallowed, or absorbed through open wounds.
- A thin-window Geiger-Mueller (GM) probe can detect the presence of alpha radiation. (This is normally called a pancake probe as it is flat and round.)
- Most other instruments cannot detect alpha radiation because alpha radiation cannot penetrate even a thin layer of water, dust, paper, or other material.
- Alpha radiation travels only a short distance (a few inches) in air, but is not an external hazard.
- Alpha radiation is not able to penetrate clothing.

Examples of some alpha emitters: radium, radon, uranium, thorium.

Beta radiation is a light, short-range particle and is actually an ejected electron. Some characteristics include:

- Beta radiation may travel several feet in air and is moderately penetrating.
- Beta radiation can penetrate human skin to the "germinal layer," where new skin cells are produced. If high levels of beta-emitting contaminants are allowed to remain on the skin for a prolonged period of time, they may cause skin injury. This is generally called a "Beta Burn."
- Beta-emitting contaminants may be harmful if deposited internally.
- Most beta emitters can be detected with a survey instrument and a thin-window GM probe ("pancake" type). Some beta emitters, however, produce very low-energy, poorly penetrating radiation that may be difficult or impossible to detect. Examples of these difficult-to-detect beta emitters are hydrogen-3 (tritium), carbon-14, and sulfur-35.
- Clothing provides protection against beta radiation.

Examples of some pure beta emitters: strontium-90, carbon-14, tritium, and sulfur-35.

Gamma radiation is highly penetrating electromagnetic radiation. Some characteristics are:

- Gamma radiation is able to travel many feet in air and many inches in human tissue. They readily penetrate most materials and are sometimes called "penetrating" radiation.

- Gamma radiation is electromagnetic radiation like visible light, radio waves, and ultraviolet light. These electromagnetic radiations differ only in the amount of energy they have. Gamma rays are the most energetic of these.
- Dense materials are needed for shielding from gamma radiation. Clothing provides little shielding from penetrating radiation, but will prevent contamination of the skin by gamma-emitting radioactive materials.
- Gamma radiation is easily detected by survey meters with a sodium iodide detector probe (known as a "hotdog" because it is long and cylindrical).
- Gamma radiation frequently accompanies the emission of alpha and beta radiation during radioactive decay.

Examples of some gamma emitters: iodine-131, cesium-137, cobalt-60, radium-226, and technetium-99m.

Difference between Radiation Exposure and Contamination

There is a difference between being contaminated with a radioactive material and being exposed to the radiation from a radioactive material. Contamination is when you have a material that gives off radioactivity and that material is somewhere you don't want it to be. Exposure is when that material is giving off radioactivity and you are near enough to receive it. Exposure to radiation does not necessarily contaminate you, and will not turn you radioactive.

It is simpler to think about perfume. If you are near a lady wearing perfume and you can smell it you are exposed to the perfume. You do not become perfume. If you get close enough to the lady that the perfume rubs off and sticks to your skin, you are contaminated by the perfume.

As long as the perfume is on your skin you are being exposed to it. Now if you go home someone else may also be exposed to the perfume because you are contaminated. Wash off the perfume and you are no longer contaminated and also no longer exposed.

The next issue will be how to protect you from exposure—and as with radiation it also works for perfume.

Time, Distance, Shielding

The best thing to do to protect you from radiological contamination is to:

- Reduce the exposure time—Medical effects are calculated on absorbed dose. The shorter time you are exposed, the less dose you receive.
- Gain distance—Radioactivity works with the inverse square law. This means by doubling the distance from the source, you will quarter the dose you receive.
- Put something between you and the source. Shielding will absorb and reduce the amount of dose you receive.

Potassium Iodide (KI Pills)

Another case where unscrupulous salespersons or well-meaning but confused preppers can confuse people is the use of Potassium Iodide. I have seen KI pills sold as "radiation pills" and touted as a cure all for radiological exposure.

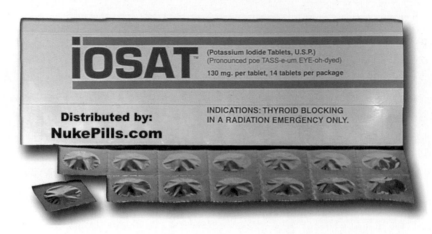

Potassium Iodide fills your thyroid with iodine so there is no room for radioactive iodine—much like an overfull spilling foam at a soda fountain. By Walt Hayes via Wikimedia Commons.

This is simply not true. KI works very specifically on one body part for one type of radiological contaminate. One type of radiological product created inside a nuclear reactor is a radioactive isotope of iodine. If a nuclear power plant incident releases radioactive iodine and you are exposed to the plume of gasses and particulates released, you will be exposed to that iodine. Additionally, if your thyroid does not have enough iodine your body will see the radioactive iodine as needed and will absorb it into your thyroid. This can cause thyroid cancer later in life. KI pills are prescribed to people who may be exposed to this radioactive iodine shortly before exposure. It does nothing after the fact. If you take it too soon, your body will use it up. Additionally, some people are allergic to it.

Nuclear Power Plant Emergencies

As a certified hazardous material technician, as well as being a radiological response trainer, I am much more comfortable with radiological incidents than a hazardous material spill. Radiation is much more predictable, and the plans for response are much stronger. However, many people are terrified of a release from a nuclear power plant and there is a lot of misinformation on the Internet. If you live within fifty miles of a power plant, plans are in place to protect your food supply in the event of a release. If you live within ten miles, evacuation routes are planned and marked. Familiarize yourself with the location of shelters, evacuation routes, and the location of emergency supplies.

Explosive

The best way to prepare for explosive threats is not to be there. If you can see a bomb, it can see you. Shrapnel can travel extreme distances and is unpredictable. In order to help create disaster awareness of explosive threats, we will focus on bomb threats and suicide bombers and give some guidance that may help reduce normalcy bias.

Bomb Threats

Bomb threats are scary things to receive; if you haven't had one before you may not know what to do. You should always follow any local procedures at your workplace, but here is some additional guidance.

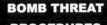

BOMB THREAT PROCEDURES

This quick reference checklist is designed to help employees and decision makers of commercial facilities, schools, etc. respond to a bomb threat in an orderly and controlled manner with the first responders and other stakeholders.

Most bomb threats are received by phone. Bomb threats are serious until proven otherwise. Act quickly, but remain calm and obtain information with the checklist on the reverse of this card.

If a bomb threat is received by phone:

1. Remain calm. Keep the caller on the line for as long as possible. DO NOT HANG UP, even if the caller does.
2. Listen carefully. Be polite and show interest.
3. Try to keep the caller talking to learn more information.
4. If possible, write a note to a colleague to call the authorities or, as soon as the caller hangs up, immediately notify them yourself.
5. If your phone has a display, copy the number and/or letters on the window display.
6. Complete the Bomb Threat Checklist immediately. Write down as much detail as you can remember. Try to get exact words.
7. Immediately upon termination of call, DO NOT HANG UP, but from a different phone, contact authorities immediately with information and await instructions.

If a bomb threat is received by handwritten note:

- Call _____
- Handle note as minimally as possible.

If a bomb threat is received by e-mail:

- Call _____
- Do not delete the message.

Signs of a suspicious package:

- No return address
- Excessive postage
- Stains
- Strange odor
- Strange sounds
- Unexpected delivery
- Poorly handwritten
- Misspelled words
- Incorrect titles
- Foreign postage
- Restrictive notes

* Refer to your local bomb threat emergency response plan for evacuation criteria

DO NOT:

- Use two-way radios or cellular phone. Radio signals have the potential to detonate a bomb.
- Touch or move a suspicious package.

WHO TO CONTACT (Select One)

- **911**
- **Follow your local guidelines**

For more information about this form contact the DHS Office for Bombing Prevention at OBP@dhs.gov

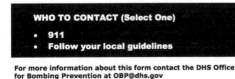

Homeland Security   2014

BOMB THREAT CHECKLIST

DATE: _____   TIME: _____

TIME CALLER HUNG UP: _____   PHONE NUMBER WHERE CALL RECEIVED: _____

Ask Caller:

- Where is the bomb located? (building, floor, room, etc.)
- When will it go off?
- What does it look like?
- What kind of bomb is it?
- What will make it explode?
- Did you place the bomb? Yes No
- Why?
- What is your name?

Exact Words of Threat:

_____
_____
_____

Information About Caller:

- Where is the caller located? (background/level of noise)
- Estimated age:
- Is voice familiar? If so, who does it sound like?
- Other points:

Caller's Voice	Background Sounds	Threat Language
☐ Female	☐ Animal noises	☐ Incoherent
☐ Male	☐ House noises	☐ Message read
☐ Accent	☐ Kitchen noises	☐ Taped message
☐ Angry	☐ Street noises	☐ Irrational
☐ Calm	☐ Booth	☐ Profane
☐ Clearing throat	☐ PA system	☐ Well-spoken
☐ Coughing	☐ Conversation	
☐ Cracking voice	☐ Music	
☐ Crying	☐ Motor	
☐ Deep	☐ Clear	
☐ Deep breathing	☐ Static	
☐ Disguised	☐ Office machinery	
☐ Distinct	☐ Factory machinery	
☐ Excited	☐ Local	
☐ Laughter	☐ Long Distance	
☐ Lisp		
☐ Loud	**Other Information:**	
☐ Nasal		
☐ Normal	_____	
☐ Ragged		
☐ Rapid	_____	
☐ Raspy		
☐ Slow	_____	
☐ Slurred		
☐ Soft	_____	
☐ Stutter		

There are many free bomb threat checklists found online. Courtesy of US Department of Homeland Security.

I have worked many bomb threats over the years; I have even taken a couple of threats at my place of work. The thing about bomb threats is to pass on the exact wording of the threat and all information. Simple things like what phone number the threat was called into helps emergency service workers determine the response to the threat. Take all threats seriously.

You need to realize that not all threats are fake, and it is not easy to determine if it is a prank, a test, or if there is a real device, so treat all threats seriously and gather as much information as possible.

Next, on a multi-line phone system, determine what number was dialed to connect to your phone, attempt to get the caller's number from caller ID, and do not hang up, even if the caller does.

Write down the exact words they used and try to note any background noises, accents, or identifying characteristics. Ask if the caller placed the device, what it looks like, why they did it. Ask them their name and location.

Realize that the authorities may want to interview you and that law enforcement may want you to help search for any devices—they don't know what is out of place like an employee or patron would.

Suicide Bombers

Here are some general guidelines to help recognize suicide bombers. Remember, just because someone has these characteristics does not mean they are a terrorist. Additionally, wounding or confronting a suicide bomber will often cause them to trigger the device. Unfortunately, even immediately incapacitating a suicide bomber may not be enough. Many terror groups create additional triggers that nearby spotters control. The best thing for the individual to do is rapidly leave the area.

Suicide bombers can take many forms but there are some general characteristics to look for.
By United States Army Alaska, Fort Richardson via Wikimedia Commons.

General Demeanor of Suicide Bombers

- The appearance of being nervous. A suicide bomber may seem preoccupied or have a blank stare.
- The bomber may not give a response to verbal or other contact because of their focus on the task.
- Suicide bombers may make an awkward attempt to blend in. Behavior will seem odd or overtly out of place.
- They don't want to be stopped, so they may avoid authority. If security is present, the suicide bomber will probably try to be inconspicuous.
- The bomber may be praying. This could include the appearance of talking to themselves. Keep in mind that many people talk to themselves, thus this behavior in and of itself has little meaning. Further, either of these behaviors could be confused with speaking on a cell phone headset.
- A suicide bomber may have behaviors that may be consistent with that of a person without any future. For example, giving away things of value, buying a one-way ticket, or being unconcerned about receiving change for a purchase.
- They may be sweating profusely that is not due to the current weather conditions.
- They may walk deliberately toward a specific object or target, often pushing their way through a crowd or around barriers.
- A suicide bomber may show a high degree of focus or intent, especially if the target is in sight.
- A bomb strapped tightly to the torso may cause upper body stiffness and lack of mobility. The increased use of backpacks may reduce or eliminate this element.
- In order to disguise their appearance, a beard may have been recently shaved or the hair cut short. There is a noticeable difference in the skin color of the recently shaved area.
- Due to religious beliefs, an Islamic suicide bomber may use herbal or floral-scented water because they wish to smell better when going to paradise.

First Steps to Making a Plan

I constantly see people spend valuable resources preparing for things that are extremely unlikely to occur while ignoring things that are likely. Because I have limited resources, I want to ensure that my time and money are spent effectively in my preparations. To that end, I incorporate the same tools professional emergency managers do when creating large-scale emergency preparedness and/or response plans. I perform a risk assessment.

Risk assessments involve identifying all the hazards in the area you are preparing for. Once identified, each hazard is assigned a numerical likelihood of occurrence as well as a numerical classification for how catastrophic it will be. I will give some examples:

A threat in my life is getting caught spending more money than agreed on projects for my website.

It is very likely (occurring at least once a month), however, it is not that catastrophic as my wife loves me and generally I can get out of trouble by telling her she looks nice. This is not a life-ending disaster, but because it occurs often I prepare by bringing home flowers a couple times a year.

On the other hand, a large asteroid scoring a direct hit on the earth is highly unlikely to happen. An extinction event of this size has thought to have only happened once in the history of the planet. It scores

Identify realistic threats, not just the ones that catch your eye.
Flickr: Lindsey Turner.

off the chart for impact, but because it is so low on the likelihood index I do not worry about it. Since I can't do enough to survive such an event I choose to do nothing extra in order to prepare.

I live on the edge of the New Madrid Seismic Zone. A 7.0 magnitude New Madrid earthquake is likely to occur at some point in the next twenty years. Some planners think we are overdue, and I have heard many experts say it is a matter of when and not if. Therefore, a New Madrid earthquake scores high on the likelihood index (but not nearly as high as my wife yelling at me). It also scores very high on the catastrophic impact index because power and fuel supplies will be impacted for up to a year as well as mass building collapse in several states. With a high likelihood and a high impact, I spent a fair amount of resources to prepare for an event like this.

Next, do a skill and equipment inventory to determine your level of preparedness. By taking an *honest* look at what you have and can do *right now*, you get a picture of where you are at in the preparedness arena. A common mistake I see people make is to shortchange the assessment process by overestimating their skills or by counting things they don't have but are planning to buy in the future. A 1,000-watt solar system is nice and you may be planning on getting it with that next bonus check, but life always seems to find a way to keep it from happening. Only count what you can physically touch. It is the same process with your skills inventory. Don't count what you have read about, saw once on a show, or were able to do when you were nineteen. Only count what you can physically do. There was a time when I was a young Marine but those days are twenty years and 150 pounds in the past.

Once you know what problems are likely to occur and you know what you have on hand to deal with them, determine what you will need to live with the problems you face. Be honest, stay realistic, but be cautious. You can never have too much toilet paper, but your wife and your insurance probably won't aprreciate you filling your attic with 100,000 rolls. Since I worry about earthquakes I know I need to keep my bookshelves from falling over. I know I have the skills to screw the shelves to the wall, and I own a screwdriver, but I know I need to buy some screws. I also know I need backup power for my CPAP machine that lets me sleep without choking to death. I own a machine that works on 12 volt, but I don't have enough batteries to get me through the night or a way to charge a lot of batteries during the day.

Now that I know my shortfalls, I can begin to address them. If I know what I need I can budget and slowly acquire the things I need to bring to me the comfort level I desire. I know I need a hardened shelter to survive a nuclear attack, but based upon the cost and my level of fear I can live without one. I do worry about dying in my sleep so I continually am on the lookout for sales on good quality deep cycle batteries.

A word of advice, preparing for disasters is not a sprint it is a marathon, a way of life. You cannot go from unprepared to master prepper in a weekend no matter how much you try. Doing so will break your bank and possibly some relationships. Steady progress is much more efficient. A written plan does much to ensure you are working sensibly and not emotionally.

As you make progress toward preparedness, you should continually reassess your progress. In my own personal journey, things that made perfect sense in the beginning became less practical as my knowledge grew.

Lastly, test your assumptions, your skills, and your plan. I bought a fancy, self-contained solar kit to power my CPAP, but it did not have the power to run my machine longer than an hour. I am glad I found that out before I needed to use it.

Planning Steps

- Determine what natural and technological disasters are common in your area.
- Assess those risks based upon likelihood and impact.
- Perform a skills assessment and equipment inventory.
- Determine your shortfalls.
- Devise a schedule and a plan for meeting those shortfalls.
- Create response plans.
- Continually reassess your threats, plans, and inventories.
- Test everything.

I find that this standard method that emergency management planners use to create large-scale plans works very well for a family. I have known people to use this method to plan family vacations. While a tornado and a trip to Disneyland are quite different, you can find similarities if you think about it.

Main Preparedness Strategies

With few exceptions most of us "preppers" haven't lived through a large-scale, long-term disaster. This means most of us are planning based upon assumptions. Those assumptions, no matter how scientific our wild guesses are, lead to a widely different set of conclusions. I applaud anyone that takes personal responsibility for their own security and do not judge their plans harshly.

I will say that many strategies are geared toward personal biases and skills rather than objectivity. Personally I like "MacGyvering" solutions. I have been jury-rigging for so long I tend to go that route first. However, more times than not I will save more time, money, and frustration by just saving up and purchasing the parts I need. I enjoy tinkering immensely, but for building a safety net for my family I have learned not to tinker. I rely on a better quality of gear.

Common Prepper Strategies

In order to help make a plan, let's discuss basic strategies and point out some complications you should know about specific plan types.

Living off the Land

I put this first because it was my first plan, and what I have now come to realize it is one of the most unrealistic. Many of my friends and co-workers are avid outdoorsmen. They live for hunting seasons. They have skill, tools, and experience. They also go into the woods and come out empty-handed much more than they ever bag a deer.

In my book, *The Prepper's Guide to Foraging,* I did the math and found that America only has seven acres of land per resident, but conservative estimates claim it takes at least ten square miles to survive on a hunter-gatherer lifestyle. That's not enough land, especially considering much of that land is parking lots and not suitable for berry picking. Couple that with all those that already know how to hunt and the available hunting land will be picked clean very rapidly.

Bugging Out

Similar to going mountain man in the example above, many people preparing for disasters plan on "bugging out" by leaving their homes in urban areas and retreating to safety in less populated areas. This is what you commonly see on television and in the movies. In fact, in the popular series *The Walking Dead*, the heroes spend much of their time in the first few seasons blindly bugging out in hopes of finding a better life in other places.

I can tell you that while the vast majority of the rural folks I know are great people, they are pretty territorial and won't share their favorite fishing hole or deer stand even in the best of times. They would probably kill over the same spot if it were how they fed their families in a crisis.

If you leave your home, you are limited to what you can carry and you become a refugee without connections and friends. From experience in helping plan mass evacuations I can also tell you that if you don't leave early you run a very good chance of getting stuck and having to leave your vehicle and go on foot.

As a side note, I would caution you about the type of bug out gear you have. You don't want to look too militant or too affluent, but you also don't want to look like a homeless person. Personally, if my area was in the beginning stages of a disaster and a guy in a business suit was walking through my neighborhood carrying a backpack, he would probably go unnoticed, but the same guy in urban camouflage and carrying an

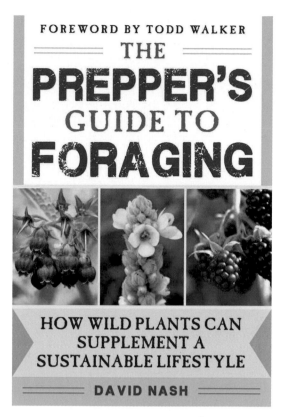

The Prepper's Guide to Foraging.
Photo by the author.

Bugging out is a common, but problematic strategy.
Photo courtesy of iStock.com/dorioconnell.

AR-15 would definitely be noticed. You have to look at your own area to decide what and how to carry your gear, but you do not want to look like a threat or a target.

Bugging In

Totally opposite from bugging out is bugging in. In this case, you hunker down, lock the door, and stay where you are. If you are well prepared this is not a bad strategy. It is actually one of two main techniques the government recommends for many types of disasters. It is closely tied to sheltering in place.

A problem with bugging in can occur if you are more prepared than your neighbors. It's not spoken of often outside of prepping circles, but the entire concept of the "zombie apocalypse" is a cover for being prepared not only for a catastrophic disaster but for the hordes of formerly friendly neighbors that are driven mad by seeing their children starve while you use the resources you have prepared.

Shelter in Place

For technological threats such as hazardous material spills, nuclear power plant accidents, or criminal acts like terrorism, government entities often recommend sheltering in place. To shelter in place you would close all windows and outer doors, turn off air conditioning systems and seal the openings with plastic sheet and duct tape. This works very well for short-term emergencies such as an overturned tractor trailer hauling toxic chemicals, but over time the sealed-in nature of a home can actually concentrate the dangerous fumes and make it more unsafe than the original

If you are going to "bug in" you must fortify your castle.
Flickr: Mesa Tactical.

spill. Any time I have worked in an emergency operations center that had ordered citizenry to shelter in place, great concern was placed on controlling the situation so they could lift the order in a few hours.

Going It Alone

In a time of stress, knowing who to trust can be hard. Limited food and resources make it easy to distrust others and try to go it alone. The problem is that there is so much to do when you don't have modern infrastructure. Cooking over a fire means gathering lots of firewood. It also means hand-cleaning clothes, looking for food, pulling security duty. One man would be exhausted and ineffective in short order. Historically, once the initial deaths after a catastrophe are over, manpower becomes a resource and groups recover faster when they have enough people to rebuild.

Providing "Security" for an Established Group

I know several preppers that brag about their firearms and amounts of stored ammunition. I, too, have firearms and bullets, but it is not the central aspect of my plan. There is a subset of preppers that do not bother with storing food or building food sustainability with farming or other means. They plan on bartering "security" for food—this can mean working for a group.

It can also mean they plan on becoming a bandit and taking from people without weapons.

Going it alone is attractive to some, but one person cannot do it all.
Flickr: nicksarebi.

Be careful you have a realistic plan as most groups won't allow outsiders in after a collapse. US Navy photo by Photographer's Mate 1st Class Bart A. Bauer via Wikimedia Commons.

The problem with this plan is that it is unethical and also shortsighted. Most preppers that have stored food have a firearm or two. A bandit that tries to gain food by force will be dealt with as rapidly as a dangerous animal would be. An established group would not likely need, trust, or allow entrance of an armed individual with no resources other than a gun.

Creating a Group

This can be a great strategy; it can also be a road to stress and heartache. I have made partnerships with seemingly perfect candidates to live on my land and help me prepare a location for surviving a disaster. People under stress act differently than when they have resources. I have tried to create neighborhood watch groups and have been met with apathy and occasional hostility.

I have met and worked with some very good groups, but they seem to be rare and based upon family bonds, a preexisting community, or a great leader. Most people don't have a situation where they can bring together a team, but it is a great plan if you can build one.

Buying Your Way to Safety

This is a very common prepper strategy. People become worried about a particular threat and solve it by purchasing *things*. I see seed vaults that are sealed and packed to store for years. I once bought one. It made me feel more secure. If a disaster came I could turn my lawn into a garden and have tons of food for my family. That is, I felt secure until I started trying to turn my lawn into a garden.

When I think about preparedness groups I think of a quote from Ghandi, "I suppose leadership at one time meant muscles; but today it means getting along with people."
Author unknown via Wikimedia Commons.

The problem of buying stuff to feel good is that you rarely learn to use the things you bought. The feeling is enough for most people. A gun does you no good if you don't practice using it, a fancy ham radio doesn't work if you don't learn how to use it, and seeds don't grow without a lot of hard work and knowledge.

Moving to the Country

I am the first to say this is not the easiest solution. In many cases it is next to impossible. I want nothing more than to live in a little cabin in the woods. Living a semi-self-sufficient lifestyle *before* a disaster is, without a doubt, the best way to prepare for a disaster. Unfortunately, unless you are independently wealthy it is hard to afford land and the equipment it needs to build a homestead and/or leave an established job.

It can be done as I have known people who have left the rat race and moved to a farm. However, for most people this plan is not feasible. There is another route—one that I am exploring in an upcoming

Nobody has enough funds to purchase total safety from every threat.
Photo courtesy of 401calculator.org.

The best time to bug out to the country is years before the disaster.
By Jan Slovik, Trutnov, CZ via Wikimedia Commons.

book, *The $100 Homestead*. I am trying to build a small homestead over time and for cash by working on the weekends and devoting every spare dollar to achieving my goal of that little cabin.

Going to Your Prepper Friend's House

This is not a plan, but I mention it because as a prepper I meet people that think this is such a good idea. If I had a dollar for every "friend" that tells me, "I don't have to prepare, in a disaster I am just coming to your house," I'd be rich. Some think this is a joke, others a compliment. I take it as an insult. I choose to give up recreational time with my family, money that could be spent on extra creature comforts, forego vacations and eating out to save up for preparations so that I can protect my family against the prospect

In almost every case it is a bad idea to depend on the goodwill of others.
By Dorothea Lange via Wikimedia Commons.

of life-altering disasters. My friends talk about Titans season tickets, or concerts, or beach trips, new bass boats, and so on. I don't begrudge them any of their fun. I am not jealous or judgmental.

People have different lifestyles, ideals, and thought processes. I believe in choices and in living with the consequences of those choices. If no disaster ever occurs then I am okay with missing the "fun times" for my feelings of extra security. I can live with the missing vacations. But if I am right, the sacrifices my family makes are to secure my family's future. I will not sacrifice food saved to feed my child to give to someone that made the choice not to prepare. That is not selfish, as I do not ask them to buy me a seat next to them at the football game, especially if it would mean their children would to go to fewer games.

If you chose this as a strategy then you are deciding to throw yourself at the mercy of your friend. The best case scenario is you would do all the grunt tasks your friend doesn't want to do and have a grudging acceptance, and in the worst case scenario you would end up killing each other.

A Better Strategy

When you made your plan, you researched the threats likely to occur in your area. You should have assessed your skills and resources. Now that you have seen the basic strategies others use, make a realistic plan that utilizes the best parts of all these strategies.

While I do not think going to the woods and trying a hunter-gatherer lifestyle would do anything more than cause a slow starvation, I do think that wilderness survival training and outdoor experience can supplement a food storage plan.

Working with a group keeps you stronger, but only if you have a strong group that you trust. You do need to buy things, but you need to practice using them so you know how they work and can use your tools comfortably.

Move to the country if you can, but if you aren't able to, prepare to thrive where you are. Locate and plan for an alternate location you can bug out to if needed.

The best strategy is to stay calm, stay reasonable, and work intelligently. Use what works and stay flexible.

Disaster Kits

Creating survival kits is in my blood. Many times I have shared how my mother could not keep bouillon cubes in the kitchen because every time I saw them I took them to make tiny survival kits to survive just like my hero in the book, *My Side of the Mountain.*

My experiences as a prepper and as an emergency manager have only served to hone my belief in kits. I don't want to have to search for the item I need during an emergency. I want to KNOW where it is. By building a kit I can ensure I have *exactly* what I think I will need *exactly* where I think I need it to be.

A search of any prepper website will mention kits in some form. We preppers have our own lingo. We have BOBs, Get Home Bags, EDC Kits, LFAKs, GOOD Bags, INCH bags, and 72- hour kits. At its base, these kits are nothing more than collections of essentials. Each term leads the user to build a bag with a slightly different emphasis.

INCH Bags

I'm Never Coming Home (INCH) bags will be larger and more complex than a Get Home Bag that contains the essentials needed to walk home from work. In many cases they are trailers. My INCH kit consists of several 27-gallon totes in a utility bed pickup (also known as a bug out vehicle).

EDC Kits

Every Day Carry kits are simply things that you carry in your pocket EVERY DAY. An urbanite that works in a suit will have a different set of needs than a farmer. I work in a prison so my EDC is extremely limited. It is mostly a two-way radio, a set of keys, and a very active and observant mind.

IFAKs

Individual First Aid Kits are basic kits that are designed to render aid to the person carrying the kit. Larger kits are normally carried by whoever in your group has the most medical training. My IFAK for teaching

INCH bag kits are full of tools and are more complex.
By David Lippincott via Wikimedia Commons.

The secret to EDC is to carry every day.
By Warraqeen via Wikimedia Commons.

a gun class fits on my vest and is based around trauma. The IFAK in my Get Home bag is focused on blisters and minor injuries.

GOOD Bag

Get out of Dodge Bags are very similar to INCH kits, but the focus is on grabbing and going, where you may have more time to pack if you're leaving and not coming back. When building my home storage I kept

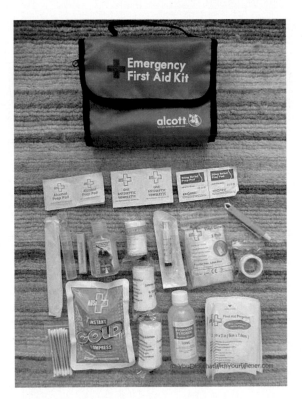

IFAK Kits aid the individual carrying it.
By vetcw3 via Wikimedia Commons.

GOOD bags are large bags but are smaller and faster to move than a full INCH kit.
By cmor15 via Wikimedia Commons.

the GOOD concept in the back of my mind. Instead of packing 5-gallon buckets with single commodities like wheat, I sacrificed some storage space to put in smaller sealed packages of multiple commodities. So it I only have time to grab a couple of 5-gallon buckets then I have a good chance of getting enough salt, sugar, wheat, etc. to make meals rather than accidently grabbing a bucket of salt and another of baking soda. I also color-coded large totes with categories. Red duct tape designates totes of a defensive nature. White is for containers that hold infrastructure items such as solar power items, candles, pumps, etc. Blue is for food and water items.

72-Hour Kit

72-Hour Kits are one of the first projects new preppers take on. This is a good idea. Coming up with items to survive a long weekend without power, water, or going to the store is both good practice and a kit that you will have the best chance of using.

There is a reason that FEMA, the Red Cross, and almost all other organized disaster organizations suggest having at least enough on hand to be on your own for three days. It takes time to get disaster response moving. Even if food is ordered immediately after a disaster, roads need to be cleared, and the trucks shipped out. I have worked disaster logistics and I made sure my 72-hour kit can last the three people in my household for at least 120 hours.

You need to rotate stock in your 72-hour kit.
Photo by the author.

A kit does not have to cost a lot of money. When I started out, I made a plan and bought a few extra items each time I went to the grocery store. It did not take a long time to build an impressive stash of items. I put an incremental shopping list in my *52 Prepper Projects* book as well as on my website. However, with a little thought you don't need anyone else's plan. Just buy what you will use.

No matter the kit, you need to keep two things in mind. The kit is for emergencies—not for the time you need a lighter for the grill or a can opener for dinner. The other thing is that you need to try out the kit. The first time I tried to use my 72-hour kit I discovered all the things I wished I had included.

Make testing your kit a family adventure. One Friday night turn off the power and the water. Live out of your kit. Don't cheat yourselves and keep notes of all the things you wish you had. Don't forget entertainment. Life without cable television is hard for some. A good book, a deck of cards, crayons for the kids makes a difference. I keep candy in mine. I have some jewelry I got at Goodwill hidden away in case a short-term disaster turns long-term and my wife feels the need to look pretty.

As you test your kit you will learn what you left out. You will rotate your stock. Batteries can go bad over time. If you test your kit a couple times a year it will get easier, your family will get stronger. It will be worth it.

Basic 72-Hour Kit Suggestions

A basic emergency supply kit could include the following recommended items:

- At least one gallon of water per person per day for at least three days, for drinking and sanitation. This is a bare minimum. It seems like a lot, but you will quickly wish you had more.
- A three-day supply of non-perishable food. Think about things that can be eaten out of the can as you will probably be dirty, cranky, and have little ability to prepare food. Include paper plates, disposable spoons/forks, and can openers.
- Battery-powered and/or hand crank radio, AM/FM radio, and extra batteries. Listen to NOAA Weather Radio.
- Flashlight and extra batteries
- First aid kit
- Whistle
- N95 rated dust mask
- Plastic sheeting and duct tape to shelter in place
- Personal hygiene items such as moist towelettes
- Garbage bags
- Wrench or pliers to turn off power/gas in an emergency
- Local maps
- Cell phone with chargers, inverter or solar charger

This is not enough, but it is based on the recommendations from ready.gov and it is a good start.

Everyday Carry Essentials

Earlier we briefly mentioned Every Day Carry. EDC is something you do without knowing you do it. We all have things we carry in our pockets every day. There are some things I would suggest every person carry in their pockets to keep them better prepared.

While EDC is a hugely personal matter, the idea is *everyday* carry. There are a lot of tools, gimmicks, and gadgets marketed as EDC gear but I bet most items end up sitting in a change tray.

As I said earlier I am strictly limited on what I can take into my work. I have a small light on my key ring and a small plastic mirror I keep in my wallet. The light and the mirror help me search small places that I don't want to stick a hand into. Other than that my EDC is limited to things my job gives me.

On the weekends my EDC expands. I add a small neck knife, a Swiss army knife, a lighter, and a Glock 19. With the ability to make repairs, light a fire, and defend myself, I feel the bases are covered. Many people would think that is either pretty light or too much to mess with. It is a personal choice dictated by your lifestyle.

When I go out to the land I keep a pair of fencing pliers and an adjustable wrench in my back pocket because I know I will need to snip, tighten, or bash something into working the way it should. I also took an ink pen and cut it to make a three-inch tube. I wrapped the tube with several yards of duct tape and then slid the mini roll of tape on a piece of paracord and tied it to my keychain as a key fob. For extra fire-starting redundancy without a lot of extra weight, I bought a pack of flints for welding strikers (a small metal tool you use to light welding torches) and drilled a small hole through the brass base of one. I threaded it into my old keychain so that I could use my knife to create sparks to light a fire.

One thing that has worked for me in the past was to buy a small aluminum pill bottle that fits on a key chain and make a tiny survival kit in it. You won't have a lot of room but it is watertight. One thing I put in my pillbox was a small amount of #0000 steel wool. This fine steel wool will spark and burn when it is touched to a battery. I have even used a cell phone battery to ignite it.

One thing I would suggest you add to your EDC is a small, rugged USB drive. In the main directory, create a file marked emergency information. Identify yourself, your next of kin, contact information, and any vital medical information you may need to have emergency room personnel know. I asked my doctor for an electronic copy of my medical records. Another thing I did was scan all my important documents—driver's license, deed, marriage license, kids' immunization records, etc. That way if something happens in the middle of the night or my home is destroyed when I am at work I at least have some records. In normal times a scan is not good enough to use for formal government interaction, but in the event of a cataclysmic emergency I am betting it would help.

Basic Food Storage

Just about every new prepper starts with food storage. Most of them spend a lot of time experimenting with different methods of packing food and trying different foods. I can't begin to tell you all the time and money I spent on methods and recipes that should never have seen the light of day. I have ruined more food than is ethical learning how to can, dry, cure, smoke, pack, and seal. However, that experimentation led me to a system that works well for my family.

Common Food Storage Systems

Before I tell you what I found to work for my family, let's discuss ways that work for others. It is up to you to decide what fits your budget, lifestyle, and needs.

Freeze-Dried Year Supply

This is the ultimate in food storage; many people I know (myself included) would love to have a year's supply of commercially freeze-dried food for each person in my family. It is probably the best option for long-term food storage, and it is very easy to use. Just add water and you have a ready meal. Freeze-dried foods have a twenty-five-year shelf life and due to the quick freeze process they do not lose many nutrients.

I have a few #10 cans of commercially freeze-dried foods, and I did toy with the idea of buying the equipment to DIY my own. At least I did until I took a bioterrorism response class where I learned that the equipment I was bidding on eBay to freeze-dry my own milk was the same equipment terrorists use to make bioweapons. Since I did not want to end up on a watch list, I stopped that plan.

My main problem with freeze-dried food is the cost. This is the most expensive option and can cost around $2,500 per person for a year's supply. This type of food is also not eaten daily so in an emergency you may have a hard time convincing picky eaters.

Freeze-dried food is the ultimate in long-term food storage, but it is expensive.
By Jaranda-commonswiki via Wikimedia Commons.

DIY Dried Foods

I love "do it" and "make it yourself" ideas. I have spent a great deal of time drying foods and storing them. In an earlier book I made a dehydrator from a box fan. I also built a biltong box from a large plastic tote so I could make South African jerky. Dried foods have been a staple food storage solution for native people and pioneers for hundreds of years. It is low tech and basically bulletproof. Every hunter I know makes deer jerky. I have made all manner of jerky and home-cured meats. Homemade bacon is incomparable to store bought. However, DIY dried foods take time to make, and don't really save money. Their shelf life is not long. Basically you should not keep homemade dried foods longer than a year. This worked for our ancestors as they needed to keep their harvest just long enough to get them through the winter.

With most of our busy schedule and the cheap cost of freezer space, I doubt many of us would be served well by buying food, drying it, and storing it just for a few months. However, its main benefit to modern preppers is the weight savings. Meat will lose much of its weight as the water is removed. It takes

Dried food storage does not have to be expensive to be effective. This DIY dehydrator was a project in my food storage techniques book.
Photo by the author.

around three pounds of meat to make a pound of jerky. With this weight reduction the size of the food also shrinks. This makes it great for go bags and camping meals.

MREs

Many people who haven't served feel that military Meals Ready to Eat is a perfect prepper food storage plan. They do have a place in some plans but MREs are not a perfect solution. They do not store indefinitely as many think. As a Marine in the post–Desert Storm era, I can attest that MREs stored in the heat quickly go bad. There are plenty of jokes about how bad military rations taste and I never had a problem with the taste of MREs, but they are bulky and contain a lot of packaging for the amount of food provided.

MREs are expensive and they have a definite shelf life. If stored at about 70 degrees Fahrenheit, they only last two years. If stored in a cool dry place you may extend that to eight or nine years. You don't get a lot of food for the size. On the other hand, they are convenient. My opinion is that they work best for 72-hour kits for short-term emergencies only.

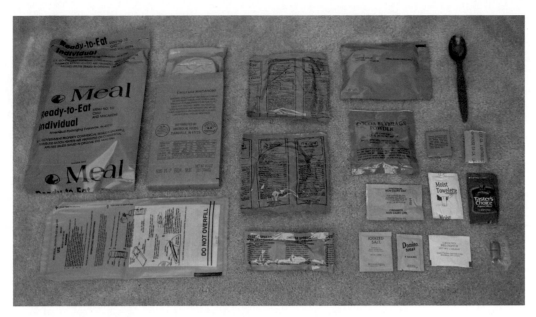

Military Meals-Ready-To-Eat can be an effective option, but they do not last as long as other food storage methods and can be expensive.
Christopherlin via Wikimedia Commons.

This is a 5-gallon bucket of wheat I processed with dry ice. Packing it yourself makes it even less expensive.
Photo by the author.

Dry Bulk

I found a local food cooperative that allows me to order dry food in bulk monthly. It primarily services those with a desire to eat healthy so there is an emphasis on non-genetically modified grains and other foods. This makes it more costly than going to the co-op and buying feed grade wheat. However, the quality is much better.

The average cost for a 50-pound bag of wheat is under fifteen dollars, or you can buy a commercially sealed 5-gallon bucket containing thirty-three pounds of wheat for fifty dollars or so. I prefer the commercially sealed buckets because the shelf life is almost indefinite if stored in a cool, dry place. You can conceivably put nitrogen-packed buckets of whole wheat berries in your well. The buckets do take up space and they do weigh almost forty pounds. I try to buy the buckets, but when money is short I spend much less and purchase more 50-pound bags and package them myself.

You can find great tutorials online that show you how to repackage bulk dry foods. I wrote about this and how to calculate the amount of oxygen absorbers in my book, *52 Unique Techniques for Stocking Food for Preppers*. Basically, you need a clean container that is safe for food and can be sealed airtight. Pack the food inside the container and replace or remove the oxygen inside. I have used dry ice to make carbon dioxide push the air out of buckets and I have used oxygen absorbers to chemically remove the O_2 from the containers. Commercial packing plants often displace the oxygen by using nitrogen.

This is a great way to make your food budget go far, but owning 1,000 pounds of wheat does not translate to food. You will also need a way to grind the wheat (discussed later), other ingredients to cook the wheat (salt, baking powder, yeasts), and most importantly the skill to cook it.

One concern with using dry bulk food for your disaster meal plan is that you can shock your system and cause all manner of digestive issues shifting from first world fast food to old world whole wheat. If you do not already bake a lot, you should incorporate dry bulk foods into your daily routine.

Home Canned Food Storage

Tools that many preppers/homesteaders/frugal moms use are water bath and pressure canners. I own several of both types and have had my share of success and failure in experimenting with canning food. Like DIY food drying, home canned items have a year shelf life. It is designed to get a farm through a typical winter not a twenty-year nuclear winter.

However, as you practice growing your own food the ability to can your own sauces, jellies, jams, and preserves is a wonderful thing. One thing you need to be aware of is food safety. Improperly canned items can allow botulism bacteria to grow and create a deadly paralytic toxin in your canned food.

The federal government has created food safety guidelines and home canning recipes that have been scientifically designed to ensure that the hard to kill botulism spores cannot survive the canning process. DIY recipes for things such as canned butter, eggs, and cheese cannot be proven to kill the spores, which is why the USDA says there is no safe way to can certain foods. If you choose to can items using recipes other than those provided by the manufacturer or the USDA, be aware of the risks.

Commercial Canned Goods

While I have some of each system listed above, I must admit that the main food storage in my home consists of cans of staples that I buy by the flat at warehouse and discount grocery stores. I have enough

Canning your own food is a step many preppers take. Be aware of the safety issues and buy a good recipe book.
Photo by the author.

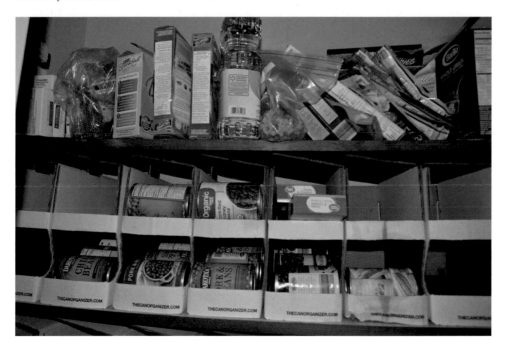

I use a cardboard can organizer to help sort my commercially canned foods. By buying in bulk and rotating stock this method is easy and inexpensive.
Photo by the author.

canned pinto beans to make chili for a battalion. A can of soup or vegetables is inexpensive, should last for years, and can be eaten cold right out of the container. Most of the canned fruits and vegetables also contain water, which can be drunk instead of drained.

A benefit to commercially canned foods is that it is familiar and easy to eat. Unfortunately, it is also bulky and heavy. If you choose to store a large amount of canned goods you need to create a method of rotation as it is easy to place the new cans in front of the older items and end up with twenty-year-old yams in the back of the closet. While it takes up a little more space than shoving cans tightly together, I use a cardboard can organizer that allows me to place my newly purchased cans at the top and pull out the older cans from the bottom so that I have a first in, first out food rotation. I buy these organizers in bulk and assemble them at home.

Mormon/LDS System

I am not a Mormon, but I do have some distant cousins that are. We do not share the same religious beliefs, but I do admire that the Church of Latter Day Saints believe that they need to be prepared for end times and should keep food storage to take care of their families.

As a group that embraces food storage they have created a thoughtful way to quickly and inexpensively stock a large amount of food. As I developed as a prepper and tried all of the methods listed above I eventually got down to basics. I like the LDS system of getting the basics first and fleshing it out with nice-to-have items later.

The base of the Mormon food storage plan is bulk wheat, salt, sugar, and powdered milk. Once you have a year's supply of each for everyone in your home you can add extras as money allows. Herbs and spices, dried meats, and dried vegetables can round out your food supply. The only problem I find with the LDS system is that it takes skill to cook from simple wheat, salt, and sugar. There are recipes for them and you can make great meals with those simple items but you need to know what you are doing.

Hybrid System

My own system is a hybrid of these. I have a little of all of the above. The base of my food storage pyramid is dry bulk food centered on the items the Mormons store. The majority of it is safely stored at my homestead. I then have a lot of canned items from my garden and my in-laws' garden. This tier also contains a lot of dried foods that I made myself. This is split between my "bug out homestead" and my basement. I have a small amount of freeze-dried commercial foods that are all solely at my land.

I keep a relatively large amount of canned goods in my pantry at home, and a smaller amount in a shipping container on my property. This is what I normally eat from. I cook with older cans and replace with newer cans. This ensures a steady rotation and that I buy what I eat and eat what I store. This is probably the best system for most people. It is inexpensive, realistic, and can be built quickly.

Using Wheat

Earlier we talked about the need to use your food storage. This is particularly true if you store a lot of wheat. You need to know how to grind it, how to cook with it, and your body needs to have adjustment time so you don't shock your intestines and bind yourself up.

You can't eat unprocessed wheat berries; you will need a grinder.
Flickr: cheeseslave.

Many people that store wheat purchase the cheapest wheat grinder they can get. I started this way myself. A good grinder is expensive and it is hard to justify spending the cost of a handgun or a car payment on something you hope to never use. However, after trying to grind wheat with a cheap hand mill I know exactly why a good grinder is an essential tool if you store bulk wheat. It is much faster, easier, and does an extremely better job.

Three Basic Types of Mills

Impact Grain Mills

Also called a micronizer, impact mills are a popular choice as they are of moderate cost and work at high speed. They only work if you have electricity and they are pretty loud. Impact mills have a chamber with concentric rings of stainless steel fins. The fins spin at tens of thousands of revolutions per minute and when grain impacts the spinning rings they burst into small pieces. This will generate some heat which is a concern for people that want minimally processed foods.

Impact mills cannot grind a cereal texture, or coarser cracked grain as they only produce flour. The flour can typically be adjusted from coarser flour to very fine flour. These mills are suitable for dry grains and beans, but cannot grind oily, wet, or fibrous materials.

The NutriMill Classic and the WonderMill are typical examples of impact mills.

An example of a stone burr millstone.
By Navaro via Wikimedia Commons.

Stone Burr Grain Mills

Stone burr mills come in sizes ranging from small to very large commercial machines. They are both quieter than impact mills and can be hand-cranked so they do not rely on electricity.

Stone burr mills have adjustable stones that rub against each other so they can produce ultra fine and coarser flour. Stone mills can grind cereal or even crack grain. Quality modern millstones are long lasting, cool grinding, and do not add grit to your flour as did the old grist mills our forefathers used.

Stone burr mills grind all dry grains and beans and some can be used for small quantities of fibrous materials such as dried spices. Unfortunately, they aren't suitable for wet or oily materials.

You can purchase both electric and hand crank stone burr mills. The Wonder Junior Deluxe Hand Mill is an example of a quality stone burr hand mill. It can also be adapted to be a steel burr mill if desired.

Steel Burr Grain Mills

Steel burr mills are built using the same basic form as a stone mill. As such, they are also fairly quiet, and have a wide range of adjustability. Unlike stone mills, few steel burr mills can grind to an ultra fine texture, but there are some exceptions. Also, because steel burrs are nonporous, these mills can grind some materials that are wet, oily, or fibrous.

An example of a steel burr grain millstone.
By Una Smith via Wikimedia Commons.

It is probably my favorite choice for a mill, and I have longed for a Country Living Hand Grain Mill for years. This model runs around $450 but it can easily be adapted to be belt-driven. I have seen many people attach these mills to bicycles.

A Few Words About Water

Many new preppers start by storing food, but as important as food is, it is a distant second to water. You can live for weeks with little food or months on a starvation diet. Without water you will die in days, sometime hours depending on your environment.

Water is something we take for granted. It is cheap and available with a turn of a faucet. It is only when it becomes unavailable that we realize how deeply water impacts our world.

The first step in dealing with the water problem is to store some. Common prepper wisdom is one gallon per person per day. I think that is too low. It does not account for hygiene only cooking and drinking. My small family consists of my wife, my four-year-old son, and myself. I plan on five gallons each day for my family. I have purchased five 5-gallon "jerry can" style water containers. This should be enough for three people to get through four or five days.

Add a quarter-teaspoon of unscented bleach per gallon of water for storage. This is a lot, and more than you would use to purify water for immediate drinking, but bleach breaks down over time so the extra amount ensures that the water is shocked and any biological contaminates are killed after the container is sealed. I rotate my water supply once a year.

Water is an essential part of any disaster plan.
Photo taken by the author.

Water weighs a little more than eight pounds a gallon. It's bulky, can get contaminated, or it can leak. This means it can be difficult to store for a long-term catastrophe. Because of this you will need to be able to get water as well as store it. Collecting rainwater from your downspouts is a great technique if your local government does not claim ownership of the rain drops. I do this, but I have also bought a bug out location that has springs. In my neighborhood I have found easily accessible creeks, and have acquired the means to both haul and purify water from them. Boiling is an easy way to purify water.

Boiling Water for Drinking

To kill biological contaminates for drinking, cooking, and washing you should bring water to a full rolling boil for one minute. Allow the water to cool before you use it. Cooling boiled water may take thirty minutes, so you may need to plan ahead.

It is important to know that boiling or using bleach only kills biological impurities; it does nothing for chemical contamination. Filtering may help with that, but the only sure method to ensure your water is 100 percent free of all contaminates is to distill it.

Bring your water to a full rolling boil for one minute.
By GRAN via Wikimedia Commons.

First Aid Techniques

We established earlier that you could die of starvation within weeks and within days from dehydration. Now let's talk about the things that can kill you in minutes. Disasters cause injuries. It's a fact of life. In normal times our medical system can perform miracles. The survival rate of gunshot wounds is upwards of 98 percent if the victim makes it to a trauma doctor in time. Unfortunately, in a disaster those hospitals and doctors may be unavailable or overwhelmed. You may have to deal with injuries that you would normally go to the emergency room for.

The thing to know about medicine is that an untrained person can allow damage to get worse by not acting, but a semi-trained individual can DO a lot of damage by acting outside of their training. Medicinal knowledge is not learned through reading or through watching YouTube. This is an area that you need to get training from a qualified source. Luckily, it is inexpensive to get basic first aid training. A basic first aid and community CPR class can be taken in a day. You can get more advanced first responder training in a week. The classes are available if you know where to look.

That being said, no book on basic preparedness would be complete if it did not cover basic first aid.

First aid involves immediate action to reduce the severity of an injury or to provide lifesaving assistance to stabilize a patient until more advanced medical care is available.

An example of reducing the severity of an injury is applying ice and immobilization to a sprain so it does not swell or become further damaged. A splint on a broken bone is another example.

Lifesaving assistance may be cardiopulmonary resuscitation (CPR) on a heart attack victim, or applying a direct pressure bandage on someone with a severely bleeding wound.

As with most other aspects of basic preparedness, first aid can be summarized as fixing what is important now. First aid training focuses on the ABC's: airway, breathing, and circulation. If compromised, the ABC's will kill a person the fastest.

Airway

A blocked airway prevents oxygen from entering the lungs. A blocked airway will cause death in minutes. It is also easy to diagnose, so like our earlier planning discussion on threat likelihood and impact, airway issues are covered in all basic first aid courses and should be dealt with first.

Unconscious Patients

With an unconscious patient, the priority is clearing the airway of obstruction and keeping it clear. Common problems with the airway of unconscious patients are blockage of the pharynx by the tongue, a foreign body, or vomit.

Most often this is done by manually positioning the unconscious person. The most commonly taught technique is the "head tilt, chin lift" method, although other methods such as the "modified jaw thrust" can be used, especially where spinal injury is suspected.

Head Tilt, Chin Lift

This technique is used to open the airway of an unconscious patient. It is practiced by tilting the head backwards. Apply pressure to the forehead while simultaneously lifting the chin. The maneuver is used on any patient where cervical spine injury is not a concern and is taught on most first aid courses as the standard way of clearing an airway.

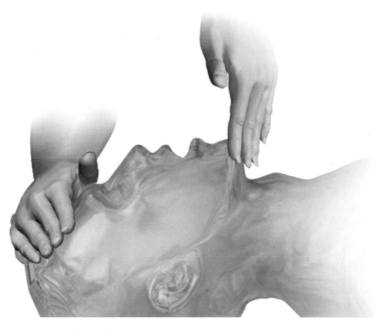

Head Tilt, Chin Lift.
BruceBlaus via Wikimedia Commons.

Jaw Thrust

The jaw thrust method is an alternative to the head tilt, chin lift technique. It is used when spinal damage is suspected, if the patient is wearing a cervical collar, or is restrained on a long spine board.

The maneuver is used on a patient lying on their back and is performed by placing the index and middle fingers to physically push the rear of the jaw up while the rescuer's thumbs push down on the chin to open the mouth. When the jaw is moved forward, it pulls the tongue forward and prevents it from obstructing the entrance to the throat.

Recovery Position

An unconscious, but breathing, patient can be placed in the recovery position to prevent suffocation through obstruction of the airway. This prevents suffocation by foreign objects and prevents the tongue from falling back and blocking the throat. It also prevents liquid suffocation by items such as vomit or blood. Vomiting (known medically as emesis) in unconscious patients is a common cause of death and it is often (but not exclusively) found in victims of drug or alcohol overdose.

Recovery Position.
Photo courtesy of iStock.com/Highwaystarz Photography.

Conscious Patients

In conscious patients, choking often causes airway blockage and they will often signal using the universal sign for choking. You may also see other signs like gasping, the inability to speak or cough, and a blue tinge around the lips.

Abdominal Thrusts (Heimlich Maneuver)

In this maneuver, a rescuer stands behind a patient and uses his hands to press sharply inward and upward right under the ribcage in order to exert pressure on the diaphragm. This abdominal thrusting compresses the lungs and exerts pressure on any object lodged in the throat and hopefully will expel the object.

Most first aid certification groups teach a tiered approach to the abdominal thrust method and alternate thrusts with back blows and show how to transition from abdominal thrusts on a conscious victim to rendering aid on an unconscious patient.

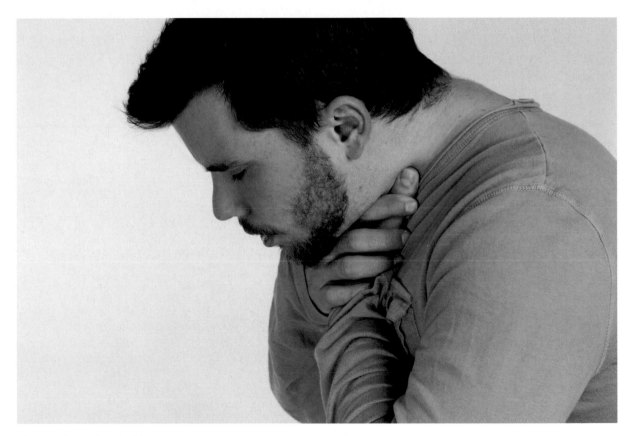

Universal sign for choking.
Photo courtesy of iStock.com/zegers06.

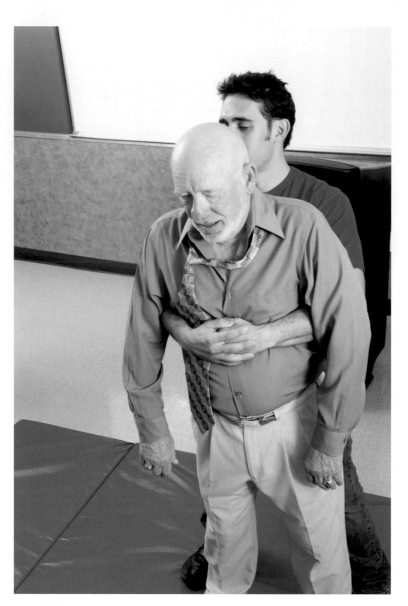

Heimlich maneuver.
Photo courtesy of iStock.com/clearstockconcepts.

Breathing

Once the airway is open attention needs to be given to find out if the victim is breathing normally. Most people take between twelve and twenty breaths a minute.

If a patient is unconscious and the airway is clear, but they are not breathing, then CPR is likely to be needed if you are trained.

If the patient is conscious but not breathing, they will most likely become unconscious very soon. Look for things such as asthma or trauma to help diagnose the issue, but treatment and diagnosis of conditions like pulmonary edema (fluid causing pressure on the lungs) or hemothorax (penetrating wound in the chest which causes a buildup of blood to place pressure on the lungs). These conditions are beyond the scope of first aid and should be prepared for by taking a first responder medical course or other more advanced training.

Checking for a carotid pulse.
By Rama via Wikimedia Commons.

Circulation

Once air is entering the blood and is placed into the blood by the lungs, the oxygen-rich blood must be able to circulate throughout the body. The most common way to check for this is to feel for a carotid pulse.

Checking a Carotid Pulse

To check your pulse over the patient's carotid artery, place your index and middle fingers on your neck to the side of your windpipe. Do not use your thumb because it has a detectible pulse and you may get your heartbeat confused with your patient's.

When you feel your pulse, look at your watch and count the number of beats in six seconds and multiply that by ten to get beats per minute.

If the patient does not have a pulse, then they have no circulation as their heart is not pumping blood. CPR is needed at that point.

Cardiopulmonary Resuscitation (CPR)

There are several organizations that provide inexpensive training and certification in CPR. The American Red Cross and the American Heart Association are the two most common. I have held certification from both, and find them to be very similar. Any person that wants to increase their preparedness level should seek out certification as the likelihood of needing to know CPR is much higher than having to deal with rogue asteroids, zombies, or other types of disasters.

For illustrative purposes, the basics of CPR are as follows:

Call

Check the victim for unresponsiveness as you don't want to call an ambulance or perform CPR on someone sleeping. A simple shake and a loud "Hey! Are you okay?" works well. If the patient is not responsive and not breathing normally, have someone call 911. In most locations, the emergency dispatcher can assist you with verbal CPR instructions if necessary.

Pump

If your patient is not breathing normally, coughing, or moving, you can cause the heart to pump by performing chest compressions. Push down hard and fast on the center of the chest thirty times. Your compressions should be faster than one per second so that you work at a rate of 100–120 compressions per minute. The chest should compress between two and two-and-a-half inches.

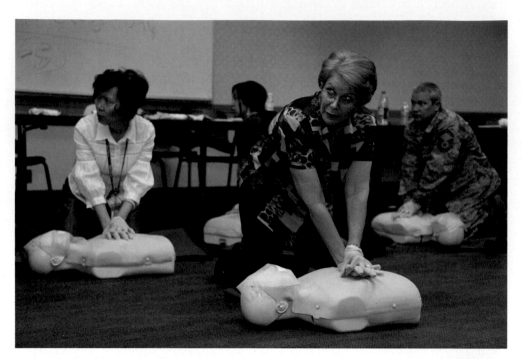

Everyone should be CPR Certified.
US Army Corps of Engineers Sacramento District via Wikimedia Commons.

Once you are sure the scene is safe, check the victim for responsiveness.
Photo courtesy of iStock.com/JanekWD.

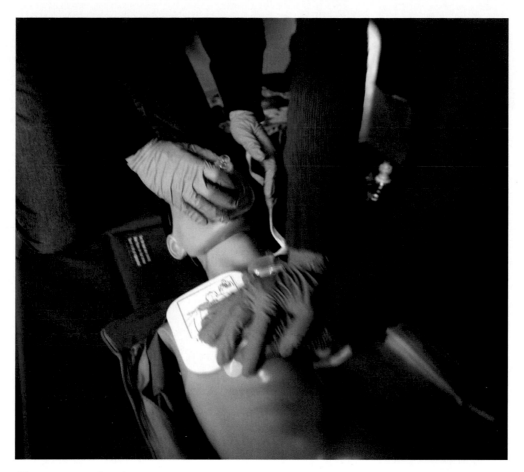

Chest compressions.
By Rama via Wikimedia Commons.

Blow

After thirty compressions, tilt the head back and lift the chin. Pinch their nose shut and cover their mouth with yours and blow until you see the chest rise. Give two breaths. Each breath should take one full second. Watch to see if their chest rises as you blow.

You will learn different memorization tools in a certification class depending on the organization. The Red Cross uses Check, Call, Care, but the basic principles are the same.

Rescue breathing.
By BruceBlaus via Wikimedia Commons.

Defibrillation

Defibrillation is becoming more common. The heart has a normal rhythm to its beat. This allows the heart to pump blood efficiently. When the heart goes into fibrillation, instead of having rhythmic electrical impulses activating heart muscles, chaotic electrical impulses cause the heart to shudder and not pump. A defibrillator identifies those chaotic pulses and then gives a calculated charge of electricity to shock the heart back into its normal rhythm. Studies show that rapid use of an Automatic External Defibrillator (AED) can save the lives of those in cardiac arrest 38 percent of the time.

Blood Loss

Circulation can also be impacted by trauma. If you have ever tried to blow up an inflatable toy with a hole in it you understand the problem. It does not matter if the heart and lungs are working perfectly if there is a wound that is draining blood from the system. This aspect of first aid is very important. As a matter of fact, in some instances, such as the military, dealing with extreme blood loss comes before dealing with the ABC's as traumatic injuries such as a severed artery can kill a person before they would die of a stopped heart.

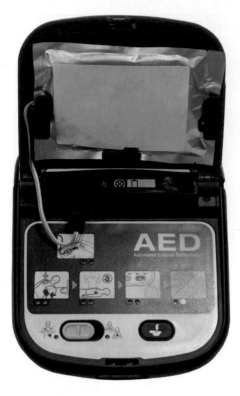

Automatic External Defbrilators (AED) are becoming commonplace.
Photo courtesy of iStock.com/Jin_Youngin.

Direct Pressure

The main way to treat blood loss is with direct pressure. If you have to deal with a large open wound, take an absorbent bandage and place it directly over the wound. Put pressure on the bandage and hold it so that the dressing stops the bleeding. Once the bleeding slows, you can wrap gauze or other bandaging material around the injured body part and tie a square knot over the wound so that it holds the original dressing in place.

If the original bandage becomes soaked, do not remove it as doing so will damage any clotted blood and will restart the bleeding. Place a new bandage over the used dressing.

Tourniquet

A tourniquet is a constricting or compressing device made from a wide band, used to control otherwise uncontrollable blood loss to an extremity. A tourniquet is placed around an arm or leg just above the wound. As the band is tightened, it compresses the flesh of the limb and closes off all the blood vessels below the tourniquet.

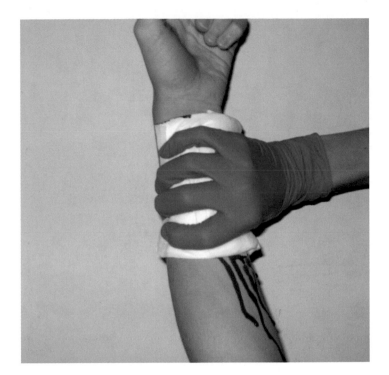

Direct pressure.
By Mike6271 via Wikimedia Commons.

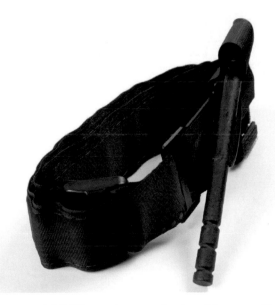

Commercial CAT tourniquet as developed for our military.
By INDNAM via Wikimedia Commons.

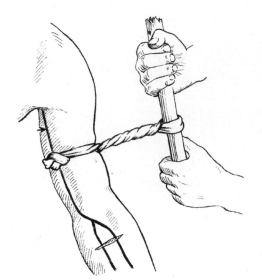

An improvised tourniquet.
By Pearson Scott Foresman via Wikimedia Commons.

While this device is extremely effective at stopping extreme blood loss, it also prevents blood from flowing to any tissue below it. This can lead to tissue death and possible amputation. A combat application tourniquet is a common item in tram kits and IFAKs as it allows people to put a tourniquet on themselves if needed. A belt can make an improvised tourniquet.

Improvised Tourniquet

To make a tourniquet out of a belt or other thick strap, wrap the material around the limb and tie it loosely. Then insert a stick or small rod (screwdriver, etc.) between the strap and the body part. Twist the rod so that it bites into the tourniquet strap and tightens it around the limb. Once it is sufficiently tight enough to restrict blood flow, use a string or rope to tie the rod against the limb so it does not unravel.

No matter the type, note the time the tourniquet was applied. It is commonly taught to write the application time on the victim's forehead using their blood.

Hemostatic Agents

Hemostatic agents are materials that stop bleeding. QuikClot is a common brand. These materials come in two common types for use in IFAKs, loose powder or impregnated in gauze bandage. Some of these agents, QuikClot for example, work chemically, while others such as ChitoSAM works biologically to bond with blood (similar to natural clotting). Earlier hemostatic agents gave off heat when used and caused burns, however, newer products such as Celox, QuickClot, and ChitoSAM do not do so.

Other Injuries

Burns

Heat is the most common cause of burn injuries, but chemicals, radiation, electricity, and excessive sunlight can also cause them. Burns are classified into degrees of seriousness, and are not only extremely painful, but can be deadly when deep or over a large portion of the body.

There Are Three Types of Burns

- First-degree burns damage only the outer layer of skin
- Second-degree burns damage the outer layer and the layer underneath
- Third-degree burns damage or destroy the deepest layer of skin and tissues underneath
- Fourth-degree burns are third-degree burns that penetrate to tendons and bone

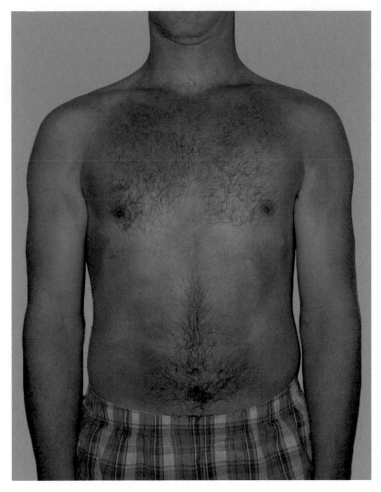

First-degree burns are the least serious.
By Bejinhan vua Wikimedia Commons.

First-degree burns are often treated with home care soaking the wound in cool water for five minutes or more and taking an aspirin. Do not ice a first-degree burn as this can cause tissue damage.

Second-degree burns blister and are more serious. Use cool water for fifteen minutes or longer to ease pain, do not pop blisters, and do not use folk remedies such as spreading butter on the wound as it increases the risk of infection.

Third-degree burns require medical care. They don't always hurt as the nerves can be destroyed. Scarring can occur.

Broken Bones

Broken bones are extremely painful and come in many forms, but these are the most common:

- Open fractures occur when a piece of bone punctures the skin and is exposed.
- Closed fractures remain inside the body and do not cause an open wound.

Second-degree burns come with blisters—this one was the result of a kitchen fire. Photo by the author.

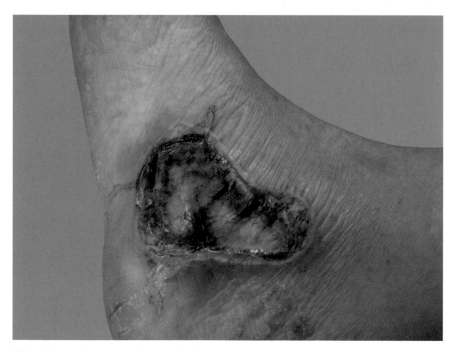

Third-degree burns require medical care. By Craig0927 via Wikimedia Commons.

- Displaced breaks occur when the bone does not remain in place—this will show in a lump in the skin or displaced limb.
- Non-displaced breaks occur when the bone breaks but remains in place so that the bone fragments remain lined up.

Broken bones heal by themselves in time; most medical treatment involves ensuring the bone heals straight. First aid is limited to treating wounds caused by open fractures, and immobilization of the joints above and below the broken bone.

Do not try to realign or reset displaced fractures, or return open fractures beneath the skin without specialized training.

Cold Injuries

Cold injuries can be deadly; hypothermia is when heat loss is greater than the body's ability to produce heat. Additionally, frostbite is the freezing of body parts. Hypothermia can be deadly, and frostbite can cause the death and eventual loss of fingers, toes, or any exposed body part.

To Prevent Hypothermia, the Army Developed the Acronym COLD

- Keep it Clean
- Avoid Overheating
- Wear it Loose and in Layers
- Keep it Dry

Improvised splinting.
Flickr: Joe Loong.

Hypothermia Symptoms Include

- Vigorous shivering
- Confusion
- Sleepiness
- Slurred speech
- Shallow breathing
- Weak pulse
- Low blood pressure
- Change in behavior
- Poor control over body movements/slow reactions.

First aid for hypothermia involves re-warming the body by exercise or body heat. Using external heat sources should only be attempted if the patient stops shivering and care is taken to prevent burns.

Frostbite is better prevented than treated. Wear gloves, and do not come in contact with liquids or bare metal. Take care during times of long-term exposure to the cold.

Re-warming of frostbitten extremities should be done slowly and should not be attempted if there is a possibility of refreezing.

Symptoms of Frostbite Include

- Numbness in affected area.
- Tingling, blistered, swollen, or tender areas.
- Pale, yellowish, waxy-looking skin (grayish in dark-skinned individuals).
- Frozen tissue that feels wooden to the touch.
- Significant pain after re-warming.

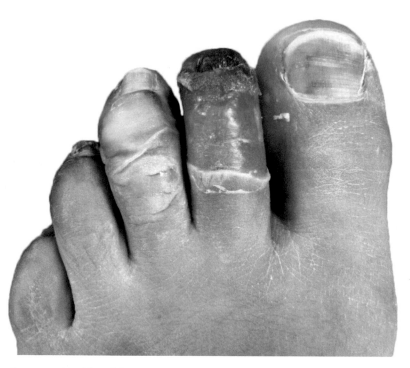

An example of frostbite.
By Dr. S. Falz via Wikimedia Commons.

Heat Injuries

Heat injuries are often overlooked, but can quickly cause death if not caught and treated.

The two main heat injuries are:

- Heat exhaustion, which can occur after exposure to high temperatures and is often accompanied by dehydration. It can be caused by water depletion or salt depletion.
- Heat stroke, a condition caused by body overheating, usually as a result of prolonged exposure to or physical exertion in high temperatures. This most serious form of heat injury, heat stroke can occur if your body temperature rises to 104 F. It can result in death if untreated.

Heat Exhaustion Symptoms

- Dizziness
- Headache
- Nausea
- Weakness
- Clumsy/unsteady walk
- Muscle cramps

Treatment for heat exhaustion is simple. You should move the patient to the shade, loosen their clothing, and have them sip water at the rate of two quarts an hour. If condition worsens, then more advanced treatment is necessary.

Heat Stroke Symptoms

- Profuse sweating
- Convulsions and chills
- Vomiting
- Confusion, mumbling—ask mental status check questions to see if brain is working correctly
- Combative
- Unconsciousness

If a person has heat stroke rapid cooling is essential. The faster the body is cooled, the less damage to the brain and organs occurs.

Remove all outer clothing, immerse in cold water or iced sheets, and fan the patient. Observe for changing mental status.

It can take months to recover from heat injuries. Once someone succumbs to heat exhaustion, they are more susceptible for months after the initial injury. Prevention is the key.

Impalement

Impalement occurs when an object penetrates the body and remains in place. It is something that cannot be treated by laymen, as removing an impaled object can cause more damage. Impaled objects have been known to sever and hold blood vessels closed. Removal can cause rapid death by blood loss.

Basic first aid is to stabilize the object without completely covering the object, control bleeding, and treat for shock.

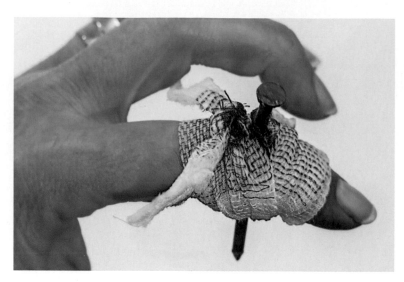

Protect the object to keep it from moving.
Photo courtesy of Max Pixel, http://maxpixel.freegreatpicture.com.

Poisoning

Vomiting is no longer recommended for treatment of poisoning. It has not been shown to help, and can cause additional damage.

Keep the Poison Control number near your phone.
Photo by the author.

For swallowed poisons, recommended first aid is to remove any poison still in the mouth, read the poison's label if available, and follow the guidance as you call for aid from emergency medical or Poison Control.

For poison in the eye or skin, remove any contaminated coverings and flush for twenty minutes under lukewarm water.

For inhaled poisons, quick removal to fresh air is the best aid possible by the layperson.

Seizure

There is a lot of misinformation about seizure treatment. The aid giver should never attempt to restrain someone having a seizure, nor should they attempt to place something in the person's mouth. Aid should be limited to staying close by and removing objects in the area that could cause injury to the person.

Remain calm and understand that a seizure does not last longer than a few moments. Comfort the patient when the seizure stops and encourage onlookers to give the person space.

Stroke

Besides rapid diagnosis, there is not much a person can do to treat a stroke outside of a hospital. Rapid treatment by a medical professional is essential to preventing permanent brain loss.

Stroke Identification Can Be Done Using the Acronym FAST

- Face. Does the face droop on one side while trying to smile?
- Arms. Is one arm lower when trying to raise both arms?
- Speech. Can a simple sentence be repeated? Is speech slurred or strange?
- Time. During a stroke every minute counts. Get the patient to a hospital ASAP.

Other Signs of a Stroke are:

- Weakness or numbness on one side of the body
- Dimness or blurred vision
- Sudden severe headache
- Unexplained dizziness

Situational Awareness

Situational awareness is vital to preparedness; if you do not have an awareness of the world around you how can you possibly recognize and react appropriately to emergency situations?

The Cooper Color Code system was popularized by Colonel Jeff Cooper, and is designed to allow a person to understand their personal awareness level so that over time they can train themselves to stay in the appropriate level as needed and to understand situational cues so that they can rapidly respond as situationally appropriate.

Colonel Cooper believed that the most important means of surviving a lethal attack was not a person's skill or tools, but was their combat mindset.

White: Unaware and Unprepared

If attacked in Condition White, the only thing that may save you is the inadequacy or ineptitude of your attacker. When confronted by something nasty, your reaction will probably be, "Oh my God! This can't be happening to me."

A quick internet video search will show hundred of assaults in which the victim had no idea they were about to be attacked, when the aggressor had several indicative behaviors that could have been recognized if the victim was more aware.

No judgment is made concerning the morality of staying in condition white; it is normal to be in this awareness level when in a safe place like one's home. However, if you desire to be prepared to react, you need to understand this level is the slowest to react from.

Yellow: Relaxed Alert

Condition yellow implies there is no specific threat present. Your mindset is that "Today could be the day I may have to defend myself." You are simply aware that the world is a potentially unfriendly place and that you are prepared to defend yourself, if necessary.

Condition White is when you are unaware of your surroundings.
By PublicDomainPictures.net.

Condition Yellow is aware and alert but unafraid.
Photo courtesy of Pexels.com.

In Yellow, you use your eyes and ears, and realize that "today may be the day." You don't have to be armed in this state, but if you are armed you should be in Condition Yellow. You should always be in Yellow whenever you are in unfamiliar surroundings or among people you don't know.

Like condition White, you can remain in Yellow for long periods, as long as you are able to "Watch your six." (In aviation, 12 o'clock refers to the direction in front of the aircraft's nose. Six o'clock is the blind spot behind the pilot.) In Yellow, you are "taking in" surrounding information in a relaxed but alert manner, like a continuous 360-degree radar sweep. As Cooper put it, "I might have to shoot."

Orange: Specific Alert

Yellow implies no threat, but Orange means you picked up on something that is not quite right. This feeling has your attention. In Orange your radar has picked up a specific alert. You shift your primary focus to determine if there is a threat.

Your mindset shifts from "I may have to defend myself today" to "I may have to defend myself from THAT person today." Orange means focusing on the specific threat which has caused the escalation in alert status.

Condition Orange means your "spidery sense" is tingling.
Photo courtesy of PeopleImages /iStock.com.

In Condition Orange, you set a mental trigger: "If that person does 'X,' I will need to stop them." Your pistol usually remains holstered in this state. Staying in Orange can be a bit of a mental strain, but you can stay in it for as long as you need to. If the threat proves to be nothing, you shift back to Condition Yellow.

Red: Condition Red Is Fight

Your mental trigger (established back in Condition Orange) has been tripped. "If 'X' happens I will shoot that person"—'X' has happened, the fight is on.

It is vital to understand that when condition Red is entered it is vital to DO something. Hesitation during times of crisis and conflict results in death.

If you see a tornado coming, flood waters rising, or a crazed man with a knife approaching—DO SOMETHING ABOUT IT!

Some, Including the USMC, have Added Condition Black

Condition Black is a breakdown of mental and physical performance. Studies have shown that when the heart beats faster than 175 heartbeats per minute, this increased heart rate becomes counterproductive.

Condition Red means you are in a fight.
By VargaA via Wikimedia Commons.

In Condition Black, the shooter probably has stopped thinking correctly.

Condition black often occurs when a person is forced to go from Condition White or Yellow immediately to Condition Red.

Anyone serious about personal protection, including the defensive use of a pistol, should study Col. Cooper's work, which has influenced much of what has become state of the art in defensive shooting.

Increasing Disaster Awareness

The best way to increase any kind of capability is to practice doing it. Becoming more disaster aware is the same way. Too often we think of disaster as something that happens to other people.

We rarely internalize threats and act proactively. Humans seem to be programmed to be reactionary.

This makes sense as we all have limited resources and we need to spend them for things we are dealing with in the here and now. Unfortunately, this can cause future problems, as little prior preparedness and the required disaster awareness can be a lifesaver.

One thing that hurts our disaster awareness and ability to appropriately respond is normalcy bias.

Normalcy Bias

The idea of normalcy bias is that people underestimate both the possibility of a disaster, and the effects of a disaster. Most people have a bias against disaster preparedness because disasters are something that

Normalcy bias is real, but you need to understand it and defend against it. Don't be in the herd when the lions attack.
By Deerstop via Wikimedia Commons.

hasn't happened to them. The idea is that if it hasn't happened it can't occur. Most humans have difficulty reacting to things that they have not experienced before. We also tend to interpret warnings the most optimistic way possible.

I once interviewed "Selco," a survivor in the Yugoslav Wars of the 1990s. He told me how normalcy bias caused otherwise intelligent people to refuse to interpret warnings to evacuate, thinking they were too smart/good/wise people to devolve into civil war. His father believed the UN would never allow things to get so bad. By the time they broke out of the normalcy bias, it was too late to get out of the war zone.

Combating Normalcy Bias is Done Through Increasing Your Disaster Awareness

- Acknowledge that disasters can occur and can impact your life.
- Identify the most likely threats to your area.
- Create a list of pre-event indicators—trigger points for action.
- I.e., if all electronics die unexpectedly, I will assume it is caused by an electromagnetic pulse and I will immediately leave and start walking home.
- Understand that bad things happen to good people, and that no one is immune to disaster.
- Avoid overreaction and worst-case thinking. Being Chicken Little is almost as bad as having your head in the sand.

The key to increasing your disaster awareness is to make the conscious decision to be proactive and aware so that you are not a victim of your surroundings, but rather someone that is aware and conscious of the world around you.

Keep your face out of your phone in public and pay attention to your surroundings.

Don't be content to look, actually see. Ask yourself what your observations mean.

For example, it is not just cold and sleeting, and because the weather has been below freezing for weeks, the roads are more likely to develop ice. It's not just raining, it's raining steadily and has been for days, and the ground cannot absorb any more water and your home is near a creek so be prepared for it to flood.

It takes effort and practice to see and become aware, but if you practice this, your life will be richer and you will see connections most others do not.

Simple Methods to Prevent Panic and Make Decisions

Panic is contagious, panic is powerful, panic kills. No matter what else occurs, panic must be dealt with before anything else.

I have held a training job that required the application of pepper spray to large amounts of students at a time. It is amazing how panic turns an unpleasant situation into an unbearable ordeal. The students that control their mind and refuse to panic can deal with the pain, accomplish the mission, and recover in minutes. The students that allow panic to control them cannot answer simple questions, render self-aid, and take upwards of an hour to recover from the simple spray.

Inside of the prison, and in the emergency management field, I have seen how powerful panic can be.

The best way to prevent panic is to make the conscious effort to willfully deny it. Many times I have thought to myself, "Self, this is going to hurt, but I'm NOT going to run" and then I dealt with the problem at hand. By deciding I was going to control my emotions, I was able to get through the situation without getting in a fight with inmates.

Colonel Dave Grossman, in his work *On Combat*, talks about combat breathing. I teach a modified version to my students before I spray them, and again when talking about calling for assistance on the radio.

Combat Breathing

Combat breathing is the simple, slow, and controlled intake and exhalation of oxygen. Breathe deeply through the nose for a long four count, pause for a four count, and slowly and deeply breathe out for a four count. Repeat four times.

This will have noticeable impact on your mind-set. You will be much better prepared to deal with an issue after an application of combat breathing.

It builds in time to think. It can be done quietly and without drawing attention.

If you are in charge and control yourself, others will notice and will increase their confidence.

If you couple this with the ability to make good decisions under stress, then your influence will grow and you will be looked at as a leader. Once you control your breathing and learn to stay calm, you can use the OODA loop to make good decisions.

OODA Loop

The OODA loop is a training concept used to explain the decision-making process and to help develop the ability to process information and make good decisions under stress.

It was developed by a young air force fighter pilot in Korea named John Boyd, and is credited with playing a large part in the success of air combat during that conflict.

The OODA loop is an acronym describing the steps needed to make decisions and stands for:

- Observe
- Orientate
- Decide
- Act

First you need to observe an event—say you are walking up to an automatic teller machine in a "bad" part of town and you observe two male youths loitering near the terminal.

You would then orientate yourself based upon your observation—are they waiting for a friend, or do they seem to be waiting to mug a bank customer? How important is it for you to get the money at THIS location?

Once you have gathered and processed the information you need to decide what to do—pick a new ATM, talk to the guys, grab your gun; these are all decisions you could make and some are better in certain situations than others.

What is important is that after you have made your decision, you should act with decisiveness and confidence. Half steps or hesitant action in interpersonal conflict gets people hurt. Avoidance is almost always the best answer, but sometimes the only real option is to fight.

When it is time to fight, it is time to stop talking and for you to dominate the exchange.

The OODA loop is important because once you understand it, and realize that all decisions run through these steps, you can use this to "get inside your opponent's OODA"—meaning, if accosted you can take action to make them react to you.

As an example, in teaching handgun carry training I used to use a video in which a bank robber runs out of a bank carrying a bag of money, wearing a mask, and points a gun at you. I'd ask my students what they thought they should do. Most would say they would shoot the robber. After some discussion, they realize it is not the time to try to draw on a cocked and sighted pistol.

The robber has already decided to take action if confronted and all he has to do is send a command from his brain to his trigger finger, while the armed citizen must see the robber, process that they are a robber, recognize the robber is pointing their gun, decide the tactical and legal repercussions, decide to draw, then draw and fire.

Long story short—action is always quicker than reaction.

But what happens if you do something that makes the attacker have to re-observe, re-orientate, make a new decision tree, and then react?

This is one reason I recommend concealed carry rather than open carry; going from, *Hey I am going to rob this guy* to *Heck, this guy has a gun* is a large leap for a criminal to make and would most likely ensure I would have a split second to take action.

Remember, there is a big difference between theory and practice, but the more you understand them, the greater chance you will survive when crisis calls.

If you understand this process, and develop a skill in using it when it is not critical, when you really need it, you have worked out your decision muscle and can stay calm, flexible, and able to act in a disaster.

Thinking About Weapons and Security

Many people begin their preparedness journey with or because of weapons. It is common for people that enjoy shooting to think of the need for self-defense. In the training world the concept is expressed with the saying, if all you have is a hammer, every problem looks like a nail.

Many preppers should spend less money on firearms and spend more on training and practice ammunition. Photo by the author.

I started my preparedness journey through firearms. I became a firearms instructor and taught self-defense for years before I started thinking about other types of disasters. I cannot tell you how many people think they are well prepared because they have x number of AR-15s and y thousands of rounds.

Unfortunately, many of these would-be preppers have no food, and little training. When bluntly asked, many of these people admit their plan is to take what they need. Preparing to be a bandit is not the way to prepare for disasters.

Basic preparedness should not be an arms race, or an excuse to engage in fantasies of world domination. I have worked dozens of large-scale disasters, and can only recall one time that weapons were needed. That was when state troopers were used in shelters because gang members from Louisiana decided to threaten force to get additional meals.

This does not mean that firearms have no place in disaster preparedness. Actually, I believe that one cannot be prepared for any disaster if they are not prepared, equipped, and trained, to use force for self protection. Firearms are a vital preparedness tool; without them, you have no chance against the prepper bandits with tricked-out AR-15s and no food.

However, it is my experience that almost all disasters will involve a functioning government, and such a government will come down brutally hard on individuals that take the opportunity to dress in military-style uniforms and openly carry weapons larger than a typical handgun.

My get home bag does include firearms, but they are all common to hunters and the average citizen, my clothes are normal blue collar worker garb, and my boots and pack are common and well broken in. Imagine how you would react to seeing a single man or a small group of strangers walking though your neighborhood in camouflage utilities and AR-15 and AK-47 rifles? Personally, I would take up a covered position and put my crosshairs on the group until they either left or I confronted them.

Weapons and security are important, but common sense and balance are even more important.

Own a gun, and get some training. Store more ammunition than you have firearms. Buy more food, better tools, warm clothes, and some communication equipment. Then, once the basics are covered, buy a better gun, take more training, and store more ammo.

Prepare in steps, stay balanced, and think about all aspects of your plan and how it would work in real life.

Think about common calibers that are always available, get guns that are compatible. I no longer lust after the newest, coolest gun; I try to buy common firearms.

9mm Glocks, .38/357 revolvers, 12-gauge shotguns, AR-15s (or AK's for those inclined) hunting rifles in common hunting calibers (.308, 30-06, 270, 30-30, for example) are also good.

Get spare parts, get good training, and practice. This is much more essential that having a $3,000 AR rifle that you can't shoot accurately.

Personally, I try for 1,000 rounds of ammunition for each disaster gun I own. This isn't enough to go to war, but it should be plenty for common use with a little extra for training. This is a bare minimum number as you need to realize a single class with a quality instructor will use that much ammunition.

Working in a Preparedness Team

If the world as we know it collapses, it's not only about survival. Once your survival needs are met, you're going to have to rebuild and to continue on with your life. Having a group of people you trust with you makes that a lot easier.

The problem is that each person I add to my retreat would seem to lower my safety margin by requiring more supplies. Fortunately, this is only true if my supply amount is fixed. My one year supply of food for my small family of three becomes a six-month supply if three people are added. I have a mother and father, plus a sister, her husband, and their six kids. Suddenly my nice cushion of supplies turns into a few months supply.

However, if those people I add to my retreat bring their own supplies with them, it dramatically increases my safety margin. In a large-scale societal collapse it is safe to assume that in the beginning mouths to feed is a liability, but after the initial period, those same mouths provide a workforce, a brain trust, and a security team.

No one person can do it all, and even if you could no one has enough time to get all the disaster-required tasks complete.

Can you cut enough wood to keep the cooking fire burning, while scrounging food, cooking it, hauling water, building shelter, patrolling for situational awareness, and then stay up all night on watch? No, you can't—no one can. A team can do this and more.

The problem with a team is building the right one. Everyone thinks they can get along, and they probably can when things aren't stressful, but add in fear, uncertainty, discomfort, hunger, and stress, and it becomes a different group of people.

It is imperative you carefully select a team that is compatible and that is willing to sacrifice for the good of everyone. There have been countless studies on how teams form and I have taken some graduate level courses on that process. In my opinion the military gets it right—they don't look for common beliefs, they look for common values. They build trust among the team members, have a common purpose, constantly test themselves, and deliberately work with introduced stressors.

In my unit, we had conservatives and liberals, cowboys and city boys, lifers and slackers, but we all were dedicated to our cultural values of Honor, Courage, and Commitment. We did not want to let the team down, or be the weakest link.

It takes time to identify people with common values because anyone can talk about values that they don't actually hold. How many people are on social media talking about their wonderful relationships while chasing every available member of the opposite sex?

Values are important, but so are skills. I still think values are more important, but no team needs all muscle and no brains, or all shooters and no doctor. A perfect team would be like a special forces A-team—highly motivated and team dedicated, with all members having a base skill set, and each one having some needed specialty.

It is unrealistic to think you can find a trauma surgeon, a sniper, a master gardener, and an engineer all willing to join your group. We just don't function in society with that wide a range of friends; however, you can find a nurse, a gardener, a car mechanic, and a former infantryman in almost every social circle.

Be selective, be discrete, and be on the lookout for users that are poison in a group.

A good team takes time to build, which means you should start now.

In building a team, you should know your area and move slowly. Giving lectures on disaster preparedness as the new owner of a rural homestead may seem like a good idea to show your expertise, but chances are your neighbors are lifelong farmers and have been living those concepts their entire lives.

Alternatively, you may expose your preparedness in a community where basic preparedness is looked on with hostility and you may be unfairly categorized as crazy, or a conspiracy theorist, or "anti-government."

If I had to do it all over again, I would not have been so quick to identify myself as a prepper online. It has had benefits, but it has also had negative employment consequences and put personal stress on relationships. Be cautions when self-disclosing your ideas and beliefs when attempting to find like-minded individuals.

A Safe Way to Find Potential Team Members

Everyone knows what a neighborhood watch is; it has little negative connotations outside of the little old lady with the binoculars minding everyone else's business. It is supported by local law enforcement and not seen as a community threat.

Getting a watch started is a safe way to take the temperature of a community in regards to who is interested in being proactive in personal safety.

Taking this a step further is a program called the Community Emergency Response Team (CERT). The CERT program is funded through the US Department of Homeland Security and is designed to be a small group of community volunteers that are trained in light search and rescue, basic first aid, and disaster assistance. They receive free training and support from the local government and, in the case of a large-scale disaster, can help their community. In turn, the CERT team will reduce dependence on first responders.

Cautious and appropriate conversations during training and team activities can easily identify the mindset of the members. With care you can build a team of local individuals that value the same things you do, who have some level of training, and that you can practice disaster skills with in socially acceptable ways.

CERT Team.
Flickr: COD Newsroom.

This is important because you do not want to be in the position of being both the community outcast, and the only identified prepper after a collapse as it can suddenly be socially acceptable to try to take from the "crazy hoarder." My dad would say, let them try, I have guns, but you can't shoot everybody, and even if you could, the consequences are terrible.

The concept of the zombie apocalypse is actually designed to be a socially acceptable method of discussing how to kill masses of people that are not prepared and are willing to kill you for your stuff.

To me, being an upstanding community volunteer that has training, skills, and social backing is a much better way to survive a collapse. Suddenly, you are not a crazy prepper, you are a community leader that happens to have some extra seeds and garden tools you "found in your basement." Now you are not a threat, but a community asset. A community tends to protect their assets.

It is definitely worth the effort to build a team, but sometimes that is just not possible. If you cannot find members you can trust, it is best to be tight-lipped and not spread information about your preparedness.

Whether you can find a team or not, you always have family, and getting your family to understand prepping is vital to long-term security. Unfortunately, sometimes family is the hardest group to work with.

Dealing with Family and Friends Who Won't Prepare

The purpose of this section is to help communicate the need to prepare with those in your family that you want to help without alienating them, or downgrading your own preparedness plans. Learning how to deal with family that doesn't understand prepping is as important as learning how to prep.

I work in corrections and know that bad things can happen to good people; I've seen the results of people-caused disasters, as well as the impact of natural disasters. I gravitate toward being ready for bad things rather than hoping they don't happen. Due to this ingrained need to be prepared, and my avid gun ownership, a former mother-in-law of mine delighted in calling me "Sergeant Tackleberry" from the *Police Academy* movies. To her this was an insult; she was unreachable and would rather buy timeshares of vacation property than spend money on a basic 72-hour kit. That worked for her, and I don't judge her, but she would not be "come live with me if the shit ever did hit the fan" as she believed. Other members of my family have thought my preparations were a "phase" or some harmless idiosyncrasy. One group you are able to reach, the other you cannot. It is wise to know the difference and to not waste resources on those that will never understand the need to prepare.

Down through the years, my family looked at my preparations with amusement. My parents tolerated my teenage experiments with wild foods or earthquake kits. As I have grown older, and they have seen things on the horizon that personally touch them, they have begun to ask for my opinion on coming winter storms, or if they should buy gold or guns.

It's like being a firearm instructor and people ask you which gun to buy. If you do your homework and build credibility, people respect your opinions. If you take the long view and work diligently toward building that respect, those members of your family could be "converted" toward seeing the need to gain some level of basic preparedness.

While I cannot assume responsibility for them and make them prepare for disasters, I can be a role model and sounding board to help them understand the issues at play so they can build a plan that works for them.

I have a few concepts I use when dealing with family that doesn't understand prepping.

My first rule of dealing with family is not to preach. My preparations are based on my needs and the things that I believe are important. Each person has their own priorities, and preaching that you are right and they are wrong only pushes them away from the direction you need them to go.

My second is never to prepare for a particular event. I am sure there is still a lot of rotting food out there that was bought in bulk specifically for Y2K, and some preppers believe they were tricked and that prepping for Y2K was a waste of money. I tell my family that my food storage can be used for Y2K, Armageddon, TEOTWAWKI, pandemic flu, nuclear winter, job loss, or when I just don't feel like cooking.

By having an all hazards approach and building capability and skills rather than building for specific events, my planning work gets more bang for the buck. I don't prepare for specific events and I rarely talk about it. I don't have a food storage plan, I have what preparedness guru John Wesley Rawles calls a deep larder. I have a lot of food, but it's food that we normally eat, just designed to be stored for longer term—basically a well well-stocked pantry. You may think such terms are nothing but word games, but words are powerful and changing my terms changed my outlook, which in turn changed the response I got when discussing this with family.

My last precept of helping my loved ones see the need to prepare is that if I have limited resources and time (and that's a given), then it is better to foster an appropriate mindset than concentrate on gear acquisition. I could buy my mom a Springfield Armory M-14 and 10,000 rounds of match ammo, but it would be much more effective to get her to go with me to the range a couple times with a .22 and help foster a desire to shoot and then help her choose a firearm that fits her needs and desires.

Whenever the family conversation gets around to disaster preparation I bring up concepts such as "Buying car insurance is considered a responsible action, but you don't have any tangible benefit from buying it if you never get into an accident. With having a deep larder, even if zombies never attack, I still have the food." Or as Dave Grossman has said, "You never hear of elementary schools burning down but they all have fire extinguishers." My favorite is "Noah built the Ark BEFORE the flood." I try to break everything down into manageable bites rather than cram it in and have them tune me out.

The best-case scenario is that your loved ones see the need to prepare for themselves and begin planning and preparing on their own, therefore augmenting your plan. You cannot out-argue someone into adopting your position. As Dale Carnegie said, "Those convinced against their will are of the same opinion still." What has worked for me is a quiet and consistent approach.

I love my family and want what is best for them. The best way I know to do that is to help them become more aware of the need to prepare. My goal is to foster a sense of self-sufficiency and personal responsibility, and to help mentor them through the beginning steps of basic preparedness.

Imagine how overwhelming it was when you first began to prepare, there is a *lot* to learn, and even more skills and equipment to acquire. We know that we cannot stock everything needed or prepare too much. The process of preparing is every bit as important as the items you acquire.

Researching and prioritizing is mental prep work so that when a large disaster occurs we are not comatose with emotional overload. If I coddle my loved ones and try to remove the responsibility to prepare for themselves from them, then I am doing them a disservice, and when the hard times come they may not be emotionally ready to deal with the collapse. What's worse is that making them dependent on my charity would cause strain on otherwise healthy family relationships.

Because of this, I feel it is worth supreme effort to work with my loved ones to prepare so that we can grow together in adversity and make our family bonds stronger.

A few Christmases ago I had a breakthrough when my parents asked me what they could do to prepare. We had a very long discussion and came away with a workable plan. At the time, my mother's home was a more favorable location for a long-term retreat than my own, and she was going to provide the location and storage space for most of my preps. In that plan we both win in the end.

Shortly after that discussion, our town had an unusually long cold spell. In the days leading up to it we talked more about our short-term plans and communication protocols and procedures. While we did not have to evacuate to my parents, it was nice having all the details ironed out in the event we had to.

That Christmas discussion had tangible benefits, and while a lot of things had to happen to get to the point where we could talk without judgment, it was worth it. Situations have changed and I now own a nice "bug out" location and my father lives there full-time, helping to develop it as a future homestead. I like to think that would not have happened without our talk.

Testing Your Preparedness

Iknow people that believe they are the next Wild Bill Hickok because they think they can shoot. However, they never compete, they never shoot for score, and they never use a timer to test just how good they are. Anyone can think they are the baddest man alive, but it's all talk until you test yourself.

You must test your plans.
By Jennifer Smits from the FEMA Photo Library via Wikimedia Commons.

Working on my state's nuclear response plan, we wrote some awesome sounding plans, but working in a basement office tends to lead to unrealistic ideas. To balance that, we tested those plans no less than three times a year. That kept us honest.

Testing a plan is as important as making one; it's the only way to ensure it works.

When planning a preparedness test, ensure you have goals for your test. You also need to ensure those goals are realistic.

Design a scenario based on the threats you plan for, create some ground rules, and then build in some preplanned informational injects to keep the test flowing.

An inject is a piece of information placed into the exercise to either make it more difficult, keep the exercise flowing, or to deal with a player. I used to have a coworker that made all the exercise decisions during exercises and always was the boss. He was highly competent, did a great job, and I truly respected him. However, because he was so good he was always selected to run the tests. It is not realistic to always assume the same guy will be available for emergency response. I kept adding injects where he had a heart attack so that someone else could get practice.

A good inject for a home-based exercise might be that the cell tower died and your teen's cell phone stopped working so they will participate in your exercise.

After the exercise is over, you need to learn from it. The best thing to do is to have a "hotwash" or After Action Report (AAR).

After Action Report

An AAR is an informational gathering of the participants in a exercise where they get together to discuss the exercise, what actually occurred, what went wrong, what went right, and what could make the plan better.

An After Action Report meeting is not designed to lay blame or attack anyone—if that happens people don't play anymore. It is designed to be an open discussion of how to make the plan better.

One home invasion plan at my house called for the child to hide in the closet as I covered the hallway with my shotgun and we waited for law enforcement. Good plan, right? In doing an exercise, we realized that the closet was directly behind where I was to be taking cover. That would mean in a two-way gunfight, rounds would impact exactly where I put the kid. Since it was an exercise, there was no negative other than, "Man, I'm stupid!" and "Where can the kid safely hide if this really happened?"

Once you gather the things that make your plan better, add them to the plan. By doing this on a continuous cycle your plan gets better and better.

The 72-Hour Bug In Test

This is one of my favorite family disaster exercises. In the 72-hour test you typically start on Friday evening after work. Turn off the water at the street level valve, also turn off the air conditioner, and the lights. I do not recommend turning the circuit breaker off as it can cause damage to the water heater and food in the freezer. Chain up the refrigerator and use the honor system on the lights and power outlets.

The idea is to last the weekend using nothing outside of what you have in your family 72-hour kit. This exercise is best done in the fall or spring before it gets too cold or too hot.

It is not that difficult to conceptualize, or to start, but you will find that, depending upon the commitment and the skill of the family members, this can be very difficult to finish.

After Action Report meeting.
By Kaye Richey via Wikimedia Commons.

In my experience, it starts out as a nightmare, but with continued practice it gets easier, and can get to be fun.

On Sunday evening, turn everything back on, and have a nice celebratory family meal. Then perform an after action. Let everyone contribute. For me, I never thought about kid issues, but after a while I realized that coloring books and crayons were worth the space in the kit. I keep some pulp fiction books in the kit, as well as a couple decks of card games such as UNO.

Once the initial survival aspects are met, it can get pretty boring sitting around in the dark.

Other Ways to Test Preparedness

Tabletop Drills
In a tabletop, the players sit around a table and work though a scenario based upon what they know and what they have. Using an electromagnetic pulse as the exercise, have each member of the family describe what they would do immediately after discovering all electronics ceased working. Work through the event and let everyone participate. This is a great way to begin the preparedness discussion and tabletops are normally the first exercise type done when government prepares for a large-scale event or exercise.

Tabletop Drill.
By MarylandGovPics via Wikimedia Commons.

Functional Drills

While functional drills are a little different for large organizations and governments, for families and small groups they are tests of functional areas of a plan.

An example would be timing how long it would take to prepare a house to shelter in place. Have some standards set and work to meet those standards. A great test is to see how long it takes to load the car and prepare to evacuate. Without practice it can take hours, with practice five minutes is a great goal.

Camping is a good family preparedness activity.
By Virginia State Parks staff via Wikimedia Commons.

Family Outings

Preparedness is about protecting your loved ones and ensuring they have a quality life. Family outings are a great way to balance preparedness training with fun. Growing up, we called it camping. However, these outings don't have to be just outdoors, they could be to discover the neighborhood, find alternative ways home, test evacuation plans, or just have a picnic at the closest park using only the food in your car kit. Doing things as a group is the best way to prepare for a disaster as it reinforces the family and keeps it strong.

Games

I like using games as a testing and training method. Playing "Where are we?" or "How do I get home?" with younger kids helps develop situational awareness. Having a map on the fridge and having the child identify their play area promotes responsibility and accountability while also building land navigation skills.

A favorite of mine is Rudyard Kipling's "Kim's Game," where objects are arranged and covered by a cloth, the cloth is removed, and the player has a set amount of time to observe the objects. They are covered and the player then describes the objects. Doing the same thing, but then drawing the items from memory also trains powers of observation. This "game" is played by some Special Forces and sniper schools to increase observation power.

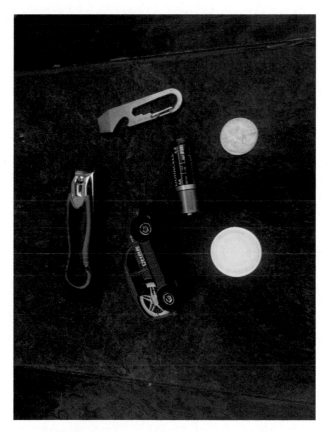

"Kim's Game."
Photo by the author.

Increasing Your Preparedness IQ

As with building situational awareness, the best way to become proficient in preparedness is to do it. Keeping the "what if" question in the back of your mind will hone your ability to deal with disaster.

The more you practice a skill, the easier it gets—remember when you first learned to drive? Every turn, each stop sign, every approaching car caused a conscious decision. Now, you can probably hop in the car and drive to work without noticing your brain making those same decisions. This is because practice builds competency.

If you want to be proficient at being disaster-resilient the best thing to do is to start preparing for disaster. It does not have to control your life, nor should it. But a few daily actions done consistently over time will allow your mind to more easily deal with the stress of a catastrophic disaster.

In the next section, you will find specific steps for achieving basic preparedness; at the end of this book you will find additional resources that go beyond those basic steps.

I visit a couple of websites for a daily snapshot of what is going on in the preparedness world, I read a book on preparedness each month, and try to do some sort of preparedness-based project each week. That is a level I can sustain without burning out, and over time it has given me a much deeper level of understanding of how to deal with emergencies.

If you want to be knowledgeable in a field, you have to work in the field. Interact with the leaders, study to gain knowledge, and above all, you must practice and do the work.

Preparedness is a journey, not a ride, and it is a marathon, not a sprint. It is impossible to be 100 percent prepared for everything, but with some effort, it is easy to become resilient against most things.

19 Steps for Basic Preparedness

Here is a basic 21-day plan. If you take what was given in the previous chapters and apply it to these steps, you will have a good basic plan that will greatly increase your base level of preparedness.

Have a Kick-Off Meeting

Meet with those stakeholders in your preparedness plan. Get the input from your spouse, children, and anyone dependent on your survival.

It is very important that after you have thought about why you want to prepare, you sit down with your loved ones and share that with them. "Honey, I love you and the kids more than anything else in life, and I worry that if something bad happened I would not be able to keep you safe. Would you help me take some steps to ensure that no matter what happens, the kids will never be cold and hungry?" will make your life infinitely easier than, "Look, you just don't understand, and I don't have time to explain it, when the mailman comes, just sign for the package, and put it in my office."

Get everyone's input. In the emergency management world this is called stakeholder support. If your loved ones feel as though their concerns were listened to, and that they have a stake in the process, then they will most likely be more willing to sacrifice in the short term for long-range results.

It is also important to get their input to ensure that you are not missing anything, that you have all the information, and that your plan is realistic. If you ignored the mind-set page, and are prepping solely for and anticipation of a commie zombie invasion that was launched after a huge solar arc wiped out the national electric grid, your spouse probably won't go along with that, so you should listen to them and compromise.

Make a Threat Assessment

Making a threat assessment is a vital part of making a comprehensive disaster preparedness plan. If you don't know what can make you have a bad day, then you have no idea how to keep from having a

"Because I said so" does not build support.
Photo courtesy of iStock.com/nicoletaionescu.

bad day. Now I know that a few pages ago I made a big deal about taking an All Hazards approach to prepping, and now it may seem that I am changing midstream, but I am not. We want our preparations to work for as many types of hazards as we can, and we don't want to obsess on a single threat to the exclusion of all others.

The more we know about what can happen, the better we can focus our efforts. During this threat assessment we want to take a deeper look at anything we are worried about, as well as anything that was addressed at the kickoff meeting. Historical information from the local emergency management agency and past presidential disaster declarations (available from FEMA) also helps. I have been trying to find a way to go to the FEMA Tsunami course they give in Hawaii, but since Tennessee is not threatened by Tsunamis I cannot justify spending any resources to prepare for that type of disaster.

Performing a threat assessment is about looking at likely threats and comparing them by how much they would impact you. This allows you to prioritize them so that you can better allocate your resources.

A large asteroid impacting the planet would kill everyone—Impact 10, but it is unlikely, so it gets a 1 for likelihood. I cut and burn myself regularly as I build projects, but it is rarely very serious, so impact 1, likelihood 9.

Look at This Chart

This is a pretty unscientific chart, but it shows the relationships. By averaging out likelihood with impacts, I can see that preparing for an earthquake or tornado is a better use of my resources than trying to figure out how to survive an asteroid impact.

	Impact	Likelihood	Threat
Asteroid	10	1	5
Cuts and Scrapes	1	10	5
Home Invasion	9	3	6
New Madrid Earthquake	8	6	7
Tornado	7	5	6

An example of Threat chart comparing likelihood of occurrence with severity of impact.

If I wanted to go really in-depth, and make a much more useful, albeit complicated chart, I could factor in the cost to prepare, and the effectiveness of such preparations. If I did that, then asteroid impact would clearly be the least of my worries, but home invasion and tornadoes would both rank higher on the matrix.

Spend some time today working on the threats that could impact your family. If you live near a highway, consider hazardous material spills, or flooding, if you live in low-lying areas.

Once you have your assessment done, you can move toward decreasing those threats as well as preparing for them if they do occur.

Mitigate the Threats

Once you have identified the threats that could impact your family, the smart thing is to reduce the impact as much as possible. In emergency management, mitigation is the effort to reduce loss of life and property by lessening the impact of disasters. Would you rather spend money on reducing the impact of a disaster, or fixing the damage after the fact?

I will give you an example. Since earthquakes are higher on my list, I ensure that the rigid connectors (such as my water heater) are replaced with flexible connectors so that the lines won't break if shaken, and that my bookshelves are connected to the wall using nylon straps screwed to the shelf, and to a wall stud.

For home invasion, or other criminal threat, I have a plan in place, a nice alarm system, and other details that tell a criminal he would be better off trying another house.

This step will require some homework. You have to know what is likely to happen, as well as what you can do to prevent it.

I would suggest that you look into the Federal Emergency Management Agency's free independent study program. They have a course called "IS-394.a Protecting your Home or Small Business from Disaster" that will explain how protective measures can reduce or eliminate long-term risks to your home and personal property from hazards.

Other resources for mitigation strategies would include your local and state emergency management agencies. Grants are sometimes available for certain mitigation strategies. After the Alabama tornadoes of 2011, my in-laws used grant funding to have a safe room constructed at their home.

While it is a larger scope of mitigation, one of the reasons the Haiti earthquakes in 2010 were so catastrophic was that local building codes were not enforced, and the local concrete was mostly sand. The same issue of cost came into play for Hurricane Sandy. Flood protection is costly, so it is almost nonexistent in New York. However, the cost of the flooding dwarfs the cost of mitigation.

Mitigation is insurance; pay a little now, and hope you never have to see a benefit, or save a little now, and possibly pay a lot later.

Prioritize Your Actions

Hopefully your mitigation steps have lessened the impacts of disasters to the point that the list of things to do is much smaller. Once I mitigated the threat of criminal trespassers by buying an alarm, a dog, and a shotgun, I didn't need to spend a lot of time worrying about it. Now I can spend my limited prepping resources on other threat types.

The next step is to take the modified risk list and look at what gives me the most bang for the buck. I can spend around thirty to fifty dollars and have a pre-made 72-hour kit shipped to my door in under fifteen minutes of Internet shopping, or I can spend half that and go to the store and build a kit specifically designed for me, depending on which is more valuable to me, time or money.

It is very easy to achieve a minimum level of preparedness. A 72-hour kit and some basic knowledge is the minimum recommended by FEMA and the Red Cross. A deeper level of preparedness takes more work, and it is important to know that no matter how much you spend, you will never be fully prepared for every disaster.

What you need to do now is to sit back down with your spouse and look at the chart and decide if you want to go after the easiest things first, or the areas that have the most impact.

Personally, I went for the easy first, both because of my All Hazards ideal, and because the small wins kept the momentum going to keep my wife on board with prepping.

Something that is very important to remember when doing your prioritizing is that you are prepping because you love and cherish your family. If you spend all your time prepping, you may be neglecting them at the same time.

I have a list of things we need to buy, do, or learn to reach that next tier of preparedness, but I also know the things my wife feels are important for our family. While I am very conscious of the dollars spent, and hate to see any money wasted when it could go to preps, I also know that spending a reasonable amount of money on family entertainment isn't going to cause us to all die during the zombie apocalypse.

Personal preparedness is a balancing act. Too little, and you are irresponsible, too much and you're a twice-divorced kook. Hitting a balance can be difficult, but it is worth it.

Assess Resources

The next thing to do, after you prioritize the actions you need to take to prepare for disasters, is to look at your resources. Typically when people hear resources they think in terms of money or "stuff." That is part of it, but time, energy, and knowledge are also resources.

You can find ways to prepare cheaply, quickly, or effectively. You can even manage to do two of these things, but except in very rare circumstances, you are not going to be able to accomplish all three at the same time.

One of my favorite authors is a man named David Gingery, whose books are about making your own metal-working tools. In an interview I read, Mr. Gingery spoke of how, as a poor young machinist, he was often presented with problems that typically were solved with $500 solutions. Gingery said since he never had $500 he had to use his mind creatively to solve the same problem with fifty dollars. I am not a machinist, and if I tried to be I would turn a $500 problem into a $50,000 problem by wrecking the machine. What I do have is the willingness to make mistakes, and a large library of books from people who have solved similar problems. That means I can leverage other people's knowledge, experiment, and tweak it to my own situation.

If I had a lot of money fall into my lap, I would use it to quickly buy the things I need to hit the level of preparedness I would be comfortable with, but since that is unlikely, I have to go slowly and prepare incrementally.

My wife and I have an understanding, so I know exactly how much I can spend without impacting our grocery budget. She trusts my judgment, and knows that I have an overall plan. So I am free to make the purchases we need without a lot of oversight, but to make it simple I have a list of the things we need for the current preparedness tiers and the next few tiers above that. This list contains how much things cost, what is a good deal, and what price is too good to pass up.

That way, if I'm at a yard sale or somebody offers me something they don't want, I can very quickly determine if it's worth spending the resources on.

You should take inventory of your skills and knowledge, not just your stuff.
By The US National Archives via Wikimedia Commons.

Remember, prepping is not about stuff, prepping should be about capabilities. Too much stuff is almost as bad as not enough. Most of the people killed in natural disasters such as hurricanes ignored evacuation orders so that they could stay home and protect against looters.

What you need to do is to determine how much time, money, and energy you are willing to dedicate to becoming more disaster-resilient. Some weeks you will spend more, and sometimes less, but pick a number you are comfortable with and stick to it.

Make a Plan

You may have been wondering why it took so long to get to the planning process, but in all actuality you have been making your plan all along. You have gathered the information needed to create a concise plan that addresses exactly what you need to do.

I used to spend hours writing, reviewing, and exercising state government plans for emergency response and recovery. As an emergency manager, I have also used these plans numerous times in a variety of major disasters. Let me just say that I believe in planning, and the process used to create a plan (all this talking and thinking you had to do to get here) is essential; when the rubber meets the road and everything starts to go catastrophically wrong, the plans seem to follow it out the window.

That situation is normal. Think about it, if you could plan and prepare for an event, and have everything in place and ready to go then it is not a disaster. By its nature, the things we prepare for are fluid and defy our attempts to prepare. That is why mind-set, skills, and the ability to be flexible in our use of stuff is so important.

I took a rearm class once, where I was introduced to the idea that when your brain believes it is about to die (and has time to do so) it will desperately search for solutions. First it looks in its mental filing cabinet for things it has done, then things it has seen, and then things it has thought about, read about, and trained for. Since things you have done are stored visually, it's the quickest to assess—that's why you hear of someone's "life flashing before their eyes."

What the planning process does is to fill that cabinet up with ideas. What you want to address in your plan are things like:

- What constitutes a disaster —when should you dig out your emergency supplies?
- What would cause you to evacuate your house?
- Where would you go, how would you get there, what would you take?
- What sorts of medications do you need to store?
- If you have defensive concerns, what would cause me to take a life?
- What happens if an emergency occurs during the week and no one is home?
- How would you get water, food, and power during an extended emergency?
- How would you deal with sanitation during an extended period without infrastructure?
- How tightly do you want to hold the information that you have some level of preparedness?
- How would you deal with hungry neighbors that did not prepare?
- How much do you need to store, and how will you fit it all in your home?

These questions are endless, and it seems the more I answer, the more questions I find to answer. It is your plan, and it is based upon your lifestyle and needs. Don't overcomplicate it, but the deeper you go, the better your plan will be.

Create a Budget

Now that you know what you're planning for, what you need, what you have, and how much you can spend to make those two the same, what you need to do is write it down into a prepper budget.

I don't get overly complicated in mine (the wife rolls her eyes at that), I just have monthly goals I want to accomplish—whether it is buy x dollars in bulk food, build something, or read so many books.

Without written goals, I tend to procrastinate or waste resources on pet projects that really aren't all that effective.

These goals are time-based and lead a clear path to where I want to be.

Your goals and mine are different. I am more into homesteading, and don't feel that I will ever be prepared enough until I have some acreage and the ability to grow my own crops. For most everyone else, a year's supply of food is probably more than enough.

No matter who you are, and where you want to take your desire to be more prepared for disaster, please realize that it takes action on your part. You have to get out and do it.

Writing down time-based goals that complement your written plan and fit within the resource allocations you have previously made is an essential part of the preparation process.

In the end, it is all about how you manage time, money, and effort in the attempt to meet your goals. You may never reach all of your goals, but the better you manage them, the more likely you will be ready to overcome whatever challenges you meet.

Build a Document Binder

This piece of the plan is something I strongly believe in because I have seen how much it can impact a family that had to evacuate or lost everything in a fire. I have covered it in other books, as well as on my website. Please think about this step, it is simple and makes life much easier.

I believe that prepping is a lifestyle, and that the actions you take to prepare for disaster ought to make your life easier. For the beginning prepper, nothing illustrates this more than an emergency document binder.

All this binder does is organize and store your vital identity documents and other paperwork. If you buy a sturdy binder and some clear plastic sheet protectors and business card sheets you can collect your birth certificates, social security cards, insurance paperwork, licenses, marriage and divorce documentation, voter registration, mortgage paperwork, and whatever other documents you may need at a moment's notice.

This makes your day-to-day life easier, as you don't have to search for records when you need them, but in a real-life disaster or other situation where you have to leave quickly, having everything in one place saves the stress of having to replace everything.

As with all things prepping, you can go as deep with this as you want. I found DVD sleeves that attach to binders with adhesive, and have begun putting DVD copies of my course material in my training

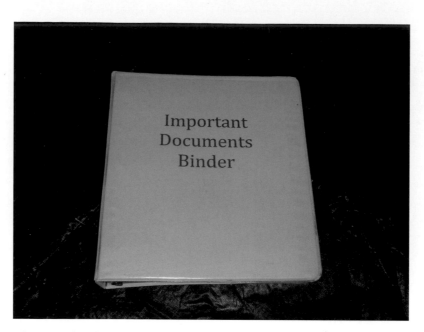

This is my family important documents binder.
Photo by the author.

binders. I can see the benefit of putting PDF copies of your documents, scans of your medical records, and digital copies of your irreplaceable family photos.

While working with evacuees for hurricanes Katrina and Gustav, it came to my attention that many in the shelters did not have their identity documents because they were lost during the storm and resulting chaos. While case managers helped them replace the paperwork. I am sure that the citizens did not need the extra stress of having to do that.

Prepping should make life easier, and this binder is the first step toward realizing that.

Organize a 72-Hour Kit

Every website on disaster preparedness, from government websites such as FEMA and Ready.gov, to nongovernmental websites such as the Red Cross, or prepper sites like mine, has a section on organizing a 72-hour kit.

The reason for this is simple—if you can take care of yourself for three days without needing outside assistance, you can weather the vast majority of situations. For large-scale disasters, it will take at least three days for the governmental response agencies to get their systems activated and in place.

During the Nashville floods of 2010, the state of Tennessee began ordering vital supplies immediately, but it took time to load the trucks and drive them in from neighboring states. In large-scale disasters, local responders might also be victims themselves.

It is just common sense to take such universal advice. So what should you put in your kit?

Obviously you need 72 hours worth of food and water, but what kind and how much? Personally, I don't use military based MREs for my long-term food storage. They are too expensive, have too short a shelf life, and when I was in the Marines I ate my fill of them. However, the convenience of them outweighs the negatives for short-term kits. They are very portable and contain enough calories that two MREs a day can keep you going. That means a sixty-dollar pack of twelve meals would last a family of four for three days.

Add the recommended one gallon a day per person allowance of water, and a 6-gallon water tote makes up a great start.

I have a pair of spare eyeglasses and prescription medicine in my kit, as well as some wool blankets, a non-electric can opener, plenty of garbage bags, flashlights, batteries, and anything else I would need to get my family through three long days.

A new pack of cards, a Hoyle card game rulebook, and some coloring books are also vital to your sanity. The iPods probably won't have enough juice to last through a minor disaster, and kids need to have something to do to prevent meltdowns.

This isn't a pack and forget it kit, you need to check the contents a couple times a year and rotate the food and batteries.

If you never check it, then the odds are that the gear will be broken, missing, or expired when it is time to actually use it.

Have a Plan to Communicate

We are a society that is built upon our communications infrastructure. We commute long distances to work, and rely very heavily on our cellular phones to conduct business.

Since our networks are built in response to demand, it is very easy to overtax the system. If you have ever noticed that you get more dropped cell calls during rush hour, you can easily extrapolate that during a crisis it is very likely that cell service will be inoperable.

However, that is not the only means to communicate. If you have a cell phone and can send SMS text messages, you may have better luck with them because texts use less data than a voice call, and your phone can hold it until it can find enough available bandwidth to get the message out.

Also, certain phone companies have mentioned that due to the way the system is designed, calls outside of affected areas can get through when calls within disaster areas are blocked.

During the Alabama tornadoes of 2011, I was able to use my cell phone to call my wife's family and pass messages back and forth when they could not call each other directly even though they were only a few miles apart.

Having a communications plan is more than deciding to become a ham radio operator (even though that is a good idea, and not as hard as many think).

Part of a communications plan is about actions, such as establishing an out of state contact person that can relay messages, and partly about learning what you can do to communicate during a disaster.

An example might be that you and your wife both commute to work, and your jobs and your home are in three separate counties. If you have a large disaster during the workweek, and you cannot communicate via normal channels, you will both head home. You may decide that if your wife does not come home within a specified time frame you will go to her, and that she could leave a special mark on her route to designate she took an alternate route so you do not search in the wrong area.

It is a good idea to have a stashed cell phone with an out of area phone number.
By Victorgrigas via Wikimedia Commons.

This could also be a nonverbal signal you can use in public to signal danger. In my rearm classes we go over the concept that you really don't want to be in a gunfight, but you *really* don't want to be in one with your wife walking next to you hugged up on your dominant hand. Maybe a signal to take the kids and "go away" might be worth talking about.

Create a Plan to "Bug Out"

In the disaster preparedness world, there are a few main schools of thought about "bugging out." Some do it as a first resort, others as a last resort, and some live full-time at their bug-out locations because they already own a homestead.

I don't have any hard and fast rules about bugging out or hunkering down. I personally feel that as long as it is safe to do so, I would rather stay at home because I have a lot more resources there than I can carry on my back. Besides that, once you leave your home during a disaster, you may not be able to come back; you also may not be able to get to where you were planning to go.

However, my house is not my primary focus, and all the stuff in it is only there for the benefit of my family. If the situation called for leaving, I would leave in a heartbeat if the situation called for it. I would not want to disregard an evacuation order and hope a National Guard helicopter would rescue us from the top of our roof.

On the other hand, I don't want to leave the relative security of my home without a plan.

When I step up my long-term food storage, I do so in a way that my food is split up into functional areas. Instead of packing one 5-gallon bucket full of wheat, I take that same bucket and put smaller bags in it, so that I would have two gallons of wheat, one of salt, sugar, and beans. That way, if I had to leave and did not have the time to sort through buckets I could grab a couple and not have to worry about accidently grabbing a bucket of baking powder, and another of salt.

I also have some large totes that have the basic function marked on them with colored duct tape. For instance, red is medical, green is camping supplies, white is defensive items, and blue is food. I don't have to waste time searching for stuff; I can just fill the truck up with one of each if I only had a few minutes to prepare to leave.

Not only does your plan need to address what to take, but it needs to cover where to go and how to get there. I hate it when non-preppers tell me they are coming to my house in the event of a disaster, and I am touchy about doing that to my friends. I have agreements with a few close friends and family that I can go to their house and they can come to mine in the event of a disaster. Some are local, others regional, and a few are out of state.

I have looked at maps to find alternate routes to their homes, and when time is available I try to run those routes in advance and look for places to rest and refuel on the way.

The last thing I can tell you is that if you think you may have to bug out, it's best to be the first one out. If you wait too long, you may find the road is impassable.

Assemble a "Bug Out Bag"

A bug out bag is not the same as a 72-hour kit; it can be larger if designed for a car, or smaller if designed to be used as a backpack. I have tried both over the years and have compromised to find a solution that works best for me. What I did was stock more items in a large plastic tote, and include a backpack. I keep this kit in my car and if I should ever have to walk home or had to leave the house on short notice I can pick and choose from the car kit and put the items in the backpack.

Alternatively, if you did not want to fill up your car with a kit, you could build a kit around a backpack and keep it stored somewhere in your home that is out of the way, but easy to access. It would be nice if it was not hidden away so that you forget to rotate your food and expendable gear, but if it is too accessible, I find that it becomes an easy place to raid for batteries when the TV remote dies, or your kid wants a granola bar.

I will caution you about the outward appearance of your kit. As I watch YouTube and browse prepper-related sites, I see a lot of folks with military-looking gear. I would not be very accommodating if, during a large-scale disaster, a couple of armed men with chest rigs and camouflage packs strolled through my yard. (However, in my state it is pretty common during hunting season.)

Depending on the situation, I can see several bad endings, from arrest to being killed for your stuff.

My pack is beat-up looking, but in good condition, in a nice, dirty dark blue. If the situation called for it, and I choose to carry a gun in the kit, it would probably not be a military-caliber rifle. I think they have a definite place in disaster preparations, but in most of the situations I can think of that have a realistic chance of occurring, it is my opinion that they bring too much negative attention for the benefits they bring. Remember, the military uses repower for suppression, and are just a radio call from resupply.

If you have ever tried carrying 300 rounds of ammo and a rifle in addition to your kit, you will find that it cuts down on maneuverability. However, a nice-sized handgun, concealed about your person, while looking non-threatening but alert, and without any ostentatious gear screaming, "Rob Me!" may be a better solution.

It is not about looking cool, or feeling like John Wayne, it's about getting to safety as quickly and efficiently as possible.

Store Water and Learn to Purify It

Earlier, when discussing 72-hour kits I mentioned that the standard amount of water recommended is one gallon per person per day. This is a universal recommendation, but depending on time of year, climate, and if you want to stay clean, it is not enough. However, when balancing the weight and size of water, with its universal use, one gallon a day is a good compromise.

We store water in a variety of ways: for utility, for redundancy, and for convenience. Our main method of storing water is to use plastic 5-gallon jerry cans. They used to sell these at Wal-Mart for around ten dollars, but I haven't seen one there in ten years. I have seen them at sporting good stores for twenty dollars, and I have a standing order with the wife to buy any she sees, whenever she finds them, if they are twenty dollars or less.

Right now I keep five of them full of water next to the washer in our basement. I consider that a four-day supply for my family of three. That gives me some extra to take care of hygiene.

I also try to take clear 2-liter soda bottles, and after cleaning out the soda, refill them, and freeze them in our deep freezer. The machine is more efficient when full, and if the power is out for a short time, the ice acts to moderate the temperature.

Whatever method of storage you use, make sure you add a little chlorine to the bottle to kill any pathogens. Use non-scented chlorine bleach, and only add a few drops per gallon. The chlorine will dissipate over time, but if sealed tightly, no bacteria can get in.

Like food, you cannot store enough water to survive long-term; you need to have a method to get water if the electricity is down. I keep extra food-grade buckets to transfer water from a nearby creek.

I also have several methods of purifying the water. Boiling works well, but it takes a lot of energy. Filters also work well, and I have several but they may not filter out all the pathogens. I have a bulk container of pool- shock that I can use to make a bleach solution to add to the water to kill bacteria.

This is one area where you cannot skimp; water purification methods are too cheap, too plentiful, and the risks from drinking unsafe water too great to risk not taking the extra step.

Water-borne diarrhea is uncomfortable during normal times, but is a major cause of death in countries without infrastructure, in crisis, or otherwise lacking medical facilities.

Store Food and Rotate It

With the exception of rearms, nothing in the world of personal preparedness has as many differing viewpoints as what is the right way to handle food storage. What to store, how much to store, and how to store the food are all things you will have to decide for yourself. There are a few different routes you can take based upon your resources and concerns.

The first thing you have to decide is what your target amount of food to store is. Three days of food for your family is the universally recommended starting point, but consider how short a time that is. There have been many winter storms that have impacted communities for twice or three times as long as that. A pandemic flu could have an incubation period of a week, and to prevent exposure you may have to stay sheltered in your home for ten or more days.

We have a target of one year for the three people in my household. However, I have several family members who may come to my house during a disaster—that three person year's supply turns to a six-month supply with six people, or much shorter supply if my parents come and my sister brings her six kids. Once you decide on a target amount, you need to decide are you going to pack the food yourself or are you going to buy it commercially. I have bought 50# bags of wheat for under fifteen dollars, but a 44# bucket of wheat packaged for storage can cost fifty dollars. Time is valuable, and there is a learning curve to packing your own, but the cost savings can be tremendous.

What types of food to store is also a decision point. We use the LDS guidelines of 400 pounds of grain, sixty pounds of beans, sixteen pounds of milk (triple if you have kids), ten quarts of cooking oil, sixty pounds of sugar or honey, and eight pounds of salt per person. This will keep you alive, is cheap, and when packed and stored properly it can last a lifetime. It is not the most fun diet in the world, however.

To help with food fatigue, we augment it with foods we *normally* eat. This adds variety as well as keeping our system from having to endure a big change. We also incorporate our food storage into our daily life to both adjust our bodies to the food, and to learn how to cook it in enjoyable ways. You can buy freeze-dried bulk food also, and I recommend doing so if your budget allows. It stores well, gives variety to your meals, and tastes much better than sprouted wheat and powdered milk. Unfortunately, it is much more expensive, and many of the prepackaged deals that advertise a certain amount of calories per day pad their numbers with a lot of wheat at inflated costs.

MREs and other shelf-stable convenience meals are also useful, but they don't last as long, are bulkier, and cost the most of any of the other options. However, for short-term disasters, the convenience offered can offset the negative aspects.

The key is to test the items you store so you pick things you will eat and enjoy, and then incorporate these items into your daily life so you are eating what you store, and storing what you eat. This helps keep your inventory fresh as well as keeping your body from undergoing a huge shock due to a change in diet.

Consider Defensive Strategies

The most controversial subject in prepping has to be guns. I am not going to get into the politics of gun ownership, and this is too short a space to delve too deep into training. There are three things I want to emphasize that are vitally important to a prepper.

- There are "preppers" (and you may be one of them) who foresee a coming disaster that will be catastrophic, and they choose to prepare for it. However, these "preppers" choose to prepare in one solitary aspect. They buy guns. If your disaster preparedness plan is all guns and no food, you are not prepping, you are planning murder. You're saying when the "shit hits the fan" you are going to go out and steal from people who have food. If you go the opposite route and have no defensive tools then you are planning to become a victim.

- Guns are tools, and not objects of worship. I like guns, as they represent equality and freedom, and I enjoy shooting them, but I don't buy them for looks, or to be cool. I buy rearms with a proven track record in common calibers. My collection won't impress my friends, and are not the newest gun featured in a magazine, but they go bang every time I pull the trigger, and shoot calibers that are common enough to be found in any sporting goods store.
- Owning a gun does not mean you know to use it effectively. Shooting is a skill, not a gift. You have to practice and you have to have some degree of academic knowledge. You do not have to spend a fortune and go to fancy shooting schools, but proper training from a skilled instructor is well worth the effort.

As a firearms instructor I have seen the difference quality makes when it comes to guns and accessories. I know that everyone cannot afford a new gun, and that any gun is better than no gun. But when students come to a class and have an extremely inexpensive gun that has not been properly taken care, they are bringing a gun that will malfunction often. Nothing is louder than a click when you need a bang. On the other side of the coin, I see students bring in very expensive guns and try to shoot cheap bullets and carry the gun on a cheap belt in a cheaper holster. They spend an inordinate amount of time fumbling around with an uncomfortable setup.

As a new prepper, if you are serious about wanting to own a gun, I would take some simple steps. First I would take a basic class. The NRA's or a state-sanctioned carry permit course (if available) are perfect. Then I would find a range that rents guns and shoot several different types of guns to get a feel for what you think is comfortable. I would then buy a gun, bullets, and a holster and belt (if it's a pistol) that are good enough quality that you can afford them, but expensive enough that you feel it.

You need something of good quality so that it is reliable, large enough so that it moderates the recoil of the cartridge, and the largest cartridge you are comfortable with.

Gun ownership is a personal issue, and I am hesitant to recommend a particular model over another without knowing a person's circumstances, but a decent pistol in 9 mm, .38, .40, or .45 works well, as do shotguns in 12- or 20-gauge, and rifles in common calibers such as .223, .308, or 30–06.

Don't Forget Lighting

In most disasters that someone could reasonably plan for, it is a good assumption that the power grid will be down. Electrical power can be an issue, but once you realize that electrical power is relatively new and that people have survived thousands of years without it, you should realize that you can survive without it as well.

That being said, the things that electricity powers are important, and lighting is something you definitely need to be prepared. If you cannot find your circuit breaker in the dark because you don't have batteries in your flashlight, then you are a very poor prepper. As with all things related to preparedness, we follow the tiered approach, and are as redundant as possible. I have a habit of buying small LED flashlights and hanging them on the backs of bedroom doorknobs. They are out of the way, very handy, and by being inside of bedrooms they do not interfere with my wife's decorating scheme. The LED flashlights are very handy, and do not take a lot of power to work, so a stockpile of AA batteries can last a long time.

We keep a high-intensity "tactical" light in the bedroom, as well as a lower power, but more efficient D-cell mag-light.

I have several camping lanterns, fuel, and mantles in my camping boxes, as well as old style kerosene lamps and lots of candles. However, if you are going to rely on flammable lighting, then matches, wicks, fuel, fire extinguishers, and smoke and CO alarms are mandatory to store also.

I have learned how to make my own candles and make simple lamps from mason jars, cotton string, wire, and old olive oil. Simply bend a wire (or paper clip) to hold a bit of cotton string right at the surface level of oil in a jar. The cotton will soak up the oil and burn with little smoke and is relatively bright. Since the majority of our lighting comes from flashlights, we store lots of batteries. I prefer rechargeable batteries, and have a small solar charger. They are more expensive, but are more economical with use.

Test Your Plan, Gear, and Yourself

I commend you for recognizing the need to become more prepared, and if you have taken the steps to get you to this point you now have a plan of action as well as the basic ability to support yourself with food, water, light, and keep people from stealing them. The next thing to do is to test your plan.

Without actually testing your plan you have no idea if it can work, and not only that, but by testing it you push your prepping skills higher up that mental toolbox so that if you are ever unexpectedly thrown into disaster your mind has a stronger frame of reference. That will allow you to better manage the stress as well as to react quicker.

There is a science to exercising plans; you don't go all out and kill your electricity and try to survive for a month the first time out. Professional emergency managers work up to full-scale exercises by first having what is known as a "tabletop." In a tabletop, all the key players sit down at a table and are presented with a problem. For example, a tornado came through town and your home was not destroyed, but the roof was damaged, and power is out. Each player will then say what they would do based upon what they have, not what they want. The key is to only use skills, knowledge, and equipment you have available. This will help identify what else you need.

Once you have done that, pick a weekend when everyone is home, and commit to having a trial run without using your utilities. That means no electricity, no heat or cooling, and no running water.

Use only what you have at your house, and set up a schedule so that someone is always awake during the night to be on "firewatch." It's not easy, or particularly fun, but it is an invaluable training tool to help you realize that you can survive hardship, as well as help you gain experience in what works and what does not.

Conduct an After Action Meeting

Immediately after an exercise, professional responders frequently have what is known as a "hotwash" or after action briefing. No matter what you call it, this gives emergency personnel the opportunity to discuss what works, what doesn't, and how to improve.

It is vital you do this at the end of your weekend exercise before everyone gets back on their iPad and returns to normal life.

Make sure that no matter what happened in your trial run, the discussion stays positive. If junior snuck in the kitchen and ate all the survival cookies, don't say "Junior ate all the cookies," but point out that maybe you need to focus on storing more food because your allotment isn't enough to satisfy, or that the rewatch needs to be more than one person. You are looking for solutions to problems, not people to blame.

You do not have to make this extremely formal, and it should not take a long time. However, if you wait to do it, chances are you will keep putting it off and valuable lessons will be lost.

Additionally, by planning, having a tabletop, having a functional exercise, and then critiquing it afterwards your brain will be "tricked" into thinking it has been involved in that type of action several times, so that if the time comes it will seem much more normal to your subconscious. That will allow you to get up to speed much more quickly.

Reassess and Repeat

After your hotwash, both the after action brief and the long shower you will enjoy after the weekend with no power, begin the process of taking what you have learned and reassess your plan. What you have learned will give you insight into making a better plan. Emergency management is a cyclical discipline, and professional emergency planners are always planning, training, testing, and planning some more.

Each cycle gets you more prepared for disasters, teaches your family to work as a group, and increases your comfort level.

Depending on your situation, what you are preparing for, and your level of comfort, you can take this as seriously as you want. But, a single rotation of the preparedness cycle is a vast improvement over the general population.

If you keep the cycle going, and are creative in your exercises (say making one into a backpacking trip, or exploring alternate routes of travel during a weekend getaway), you can make this a fun part of your lifestyle. We like to take classes, and spend our time building and creating new things that make us more prepared and self-reliant, but that's because we enjoy doing it.

Prepping should not be a chore; it should be a path that balances your life. You make an extra effort when things are easy to make tough times easier.

Closing Thoughts

It cannot be said enough that if prepping makes your life difficult, you are not doing it right.

Prepping is life insurance, it is common sense, and it should make you sleep easier at night.

Do not let yourself be bothered by the inconsequential. One has only so much time in this world, so devote it to the work and the people most important to you, to those you love and things that matter. One can waste half a lifetime with people one doesn't really like, or doing things when one would be better off somewhere else.

—Louis L'Amour

Additional Resources

This list is by no means comprehensive; I have left out some great resources strictly because this is not a book of links. All of the resources listed below are great and I personally use all of them.

Nonfiction Books
- *Making the Best of Basics* by James Talmage Stevens
- *How to Survive the End of the World as We Know It* by James Wesley Rawles
- *Tools for Survival* by John Wesley Rawles
- *All New Square Foot Gardening* by Mel Bartholomew
- *Gardening When It Counts: Growing Food in Hard Times* by Steve Solomon
- *Putting Food By: Fifth Edition* by Janet Greene, Ruth Hertzberg, and Beatrice Vaughan
- *The Have-More Plan* by Ed and Carolyn Robinson
- *The Home Water Supply: How to Find, Filter, Store, and Conserve It* by Stu Campbell
- *Crisis Preparedness Handbook: A Comprehensive Guide to Home Storage and Physical Survival* by Jack A. Spigarelli
- *Don't Get Caught With Your Pantry Down* by James Talmage Stevens
- *Possum Living: How to Live Well Without a Job and with (Almost) No Money* by Dolly Freed
- *PREPAREDNESS NOW!: An Emergency Survival Guide (Expanded and Revised Edition) (Process Self-Reliance)* by Aton Edwards
- *Basic Butchering of Livestock & Game* by John J. Mettler
- *Emergency Food Storage & Survival Handbook: Everything You Need to Know to Keep Your Family Safe in a Crisis* by Peggy Layton
- *The Complete Family Guide to Natural Home Remedies: Safe and Effective Treatments for Common Ailments (Illustrated Health Reference)* by C. Norman Shealy
- *Emergency War Surgery* by Dr. Martin Fackler, et al.

- *Ditch Medicine: Advanced Field Procedures For Emergencies* by Hugh Coffee
- *Adventure Medical Kits: A Comprehensive Guide to Wilderness & Travel Medicine* by Eric A. Weiss, M.D.
- *Wilderness Medicine, 5th Edition* by Paul S. Auerbach
- *Where There Is No Vet* by Bill Forse
- *Guide to Emergency Survival Communications* by Dave Ingram
- *Art of War* by Sun Tzu
- *Total Resistance* by Major H. von Dach
- *In the Gravest Extreme: The Role of the Firearm in Personal Protection* by Massad F. Ayoob
- *Ayoob Files: The Book* by Massad F. Ayoob
- *Boy Scouts Handbook: The First Edition, 1911*
- *Essential Bushcraft* by Ray Mears
- *The Foxfire Book* series
- *SAS Urban Survival Handbook* by John "Lofty" Wiseman
- *Tom Brown's Field Guide to Nature Observation and Tracking* by Tom Brown Jr.
- *When Technology Fails (Revised & Expanded)* by Matthew Stein
- *Survival Mom* by Lisa Bedford
- *The Practical Preppers Complete Guide to Disaster Preparedness* by Scott Hunt

Fiction Books
- *One Second After* by William R. Forstchen
- *Earth Abides* by George R. Stewart
- *Survivors: A Novel of the Coming Collapse* by James Wesley Rawles
- *Lights Out* by David Crawford
- *Unintended Consequences* by John Ross

Websites
- Survivalblog.com
- backdoorsurvival.com
- Prepperwebsite.com
- thesurvivalpodcast.com
- thesurvivalistblog.net
- modernsurvivalblog.com
- thesurvivalmom.com
- itstactical.com
- permies.com

YouTube Channels
- My Little Homestead
- Bexar Prepper
- Dr Bones NurseAmy
- Equip 2 Endure
- Growing your Greens
- IraqVeteran888
- Jack Spirko
- LDSPrepper
- Michigansnowpony
- Wranglerstar
- Engineer775

Index

About the Author

David Nash is a long-term prepper, but he is also a former emergency management professional with a degree in Emergency Management. His real world disaster response experience combined with his view toward personal disaster preparedness gives him a unique perspective.

Currently, David works in the field of Adult Corrections and is employed as an Academy Instructor. He is currently developing a $100 homestead with his wife and son. They are learning just how challenging it is to reclaim a neglected hillside and turn it into a working homestead without the benefit of money or a lot of time.

David is the author of several nonfiction works in the areas of self-defense, food preservation, foraging, and disaster preparedness. You can find him online at YouTube.com/TNGun and his personal website, TNGun.com.